Kathleen

100 Successful Omani Women

Experiences, Thoughts & Inspirations
How to Empower!

presence
PUBLISHING

❋

Bibliographic information published by the Deutsche Nationalbibliothek
The Deutsche Nationalbibliothek lists this publication in the Deutsche
Nationalbibliografie; detailed bibliographic data are available on the
Internet at http://dnb.dnb.de.

❋

This title has also been published as an eBook.
E-Book ISBN 978-3-9823444-9-2

Original Edition
Copyright © 2021 by Kathleen Nejad. All rights reserved
Published by © presence publishing, Salem - Germany

Graphics / Design and Cover Design by Julia Bitschi, Austria
Cover Photo by Katrin Zeidler, Germany
Edited by Fiona Simpson-Stoeber, Germany and Irena Svetec, UAE
Printing and Binding in Oman, Mazoon Printing LLC, Muscat
ISBN 978-3-9823444-8-5

**You can find more information about the author on the Internet at
www.kathleen-nejad.com**

＊

Dedicated to everyone who finds inspiration

in the magic of successful stories

＊

Contents

Preface   8 – 9

Approach   10 – 11

Oman   12 – 13

Suad Al Lamki (in memory of)   14 – 17

Women at a Glance   18 – 21

100 Successful Omani Women:

    Adila Al Ismaili   24 – 25
    Ahlam Hamoud Al Jahwari   26 – 27
    Ahlam Jahdhami   28 – 29
    Aisha Al Saifi   30 – 31
    Alena Dique   32 – 33
    Alia Al Qalam Al Yafie   34 – 35
    Al Sayyida Basma Al Said   36 – 37
    Al Sayyida Mayya Al Said   38 – 39
    Amal Al Raisi   42 – 43
    (Dr.) Amina Abdullah Al Balushi   44 – 45
    Areej Al Ismaili   46 – 47
    Areej Mohsin Haider Darwish   48 – 51
    Asila Al Musalhi   52 – 53
    Asma Ali Al Zadjali   54 – 55
    Azza Al Ismaili   56 – 57
    (Dr.) Badria Al Shihhi   58 – 59
    Badriya Al Siyabi   62 – 63
    Baida Al Zadjali   64 – 65
    Balqees Al Hassani   66 – 67

Contents

Bothaina Al Zaabi	68 – 69
Diana Somar	72 – 73
Fathiya Al Aisari	74 – 75
(Dr.) Fatin Said Al Zadjali	76 – 77
(Dr.) Fatma Al Balushi	78 – 79
Fatma Al Maimani	80 – 81
Fatma Said Al Sulaimani	82 – 83
Fatma Sulaiman Al Azri	84 – 85
Fatma Sultan Bahwan Al Mukhaini	88 – 89
Ghaya Al Barwani	90 – 91
Hanaa Al Hinai	94 – 95
Hanaa Mohammed Al Kharusi	96 – 97
Haritha Salim Al Busaidi	98 – 99
Haura Al Wahaibi	100 – 101
Huda Hamed	102 – 103
Ibtisam Alkhaifi	106 – 107
Jokha Khalid Al Naamani	108 – 109
Kamilya Lamk Al-Lamki	110 – 111
Laila Al Hadhrami	112 – 113
Laila Al Rawahi	114 – 115
(Dr.) Laila Harub Al Kharusi	118 – 119
Lamia Al Ansi	120 – 121
Lamya Adnan Al Haj	122 – 123
(Dr.) Lamya Harub	126 – 127
Lujaina Al Kharusi	128 – 129
Lujaina Mohsin Darwish	130 – 131
Maani Abdullah Hamed Al Busaidi	132 – 133
Maha Al Balushi	134 – 135
Maha Saud Kalmoor Al Raisi	138 – 139
Maimuna Al-Sulaimani	140 – 141
Maisa Al Hooti	142 – 143
Majan Al Abdullatif	144 – 145

Contents

Malak Al Shaibani	146 – 147
Maliha Al Sulaimani	150 – 151
Maria Sarfaraz Ahmed	152 – 153
Mariya Al Hashar	154 – 155
Maryam Khalifa Al Amri	156 – 157
Moza Ibrahim Al Azri	160 – 161
Moza S. Al Wardi	162 – 163
Muntaha Al Zarafy	164 – 165
Nadhira Ahmed Alharthy	166 – 167
Nahla Al Balushi	170 – 171
Najah Al Rashdi	172 – 173
Najla Al Mayahi	174 – 175
Nashwa Al Rawahy	176 – 177
Nasima Al Balushi	178 – 179
Najya Al Hinai	180 – 181
Noura Mohammed Abdullah Al Dhahouri	182 – 183
Nutaila Al Kharusi	186 – 187
Rahma Al Hinai	188 – 189
Rawan AlMahrouqi	190 – 191
Reem Alzadjali	192 – 193
Rehab Al Lawati	194 – 195
Riham Noor Al Zadjali	196 – 197
Rumaitha Al Busaidi	198 – 199
Safiya Al Bahlani	200 – 201
Sahara D. Hamayon	204 – 205
Salha Al Ismaili	206 – 207
Salma Al Hashmi	208 – 209
(Dr.) Salma Mohamed Al Kindy	210 – 211
Samah Al Rawahi	212 – 213
Samiya Al Balushi	214 – 215
Sara Fida	216 – 217
(Dr.) Sausan Al Riyami	218 – 219
Shadha Al Raisi	222 – 223

Contents

Shadya Al Ismaily   224 – 225
(Dr.) Shamsa Al Sheibani   226 – 227
Sharifa Al Harthy   228 – 229
Shatha Salim Al Maskiry   232 – 233
Shemsa Al-Nabhani Sora   234 – 235
Al Rowas (MD, MSc) Suad   236 – 237
Al Balushi Sukainah   238 – 239
Abdullah Sumaiya Al   242 – 243
Wahaibi Taghreed Al   244 – 245
Lawati Umaima Al   246 – 247
Mahdhori   248 – 249
(Dr.) Yasmin Al Bulushi   250 – 251
Zahra Al Harmali   254 – 255
Zainab Al Harrasi   256 – 257
Zakiya Talib Al Amri   258 – 259
Zuwaina Al Rashdi   260 – 261

Acknowledgments   262 – 263

Photograph Credits   264 – 265

Imagine a world where strong, successful, accomplished women use their strengths to encourage, inspire, and nurture a mission to support their peers, and empower other women all over the globe into feeling more confident about their lives.

As a mother to three young women, this is a vision I am personally very passionate about; it is a vision I have tried to offer you in this book, a vision I personally believe is worth working hard towards achieving.

This book will reveal the stories of 100 such empowering women within Oman. The life journeys of these 100 successful Omani women will share with you the experiences they have had, the challenges they have faced, and the success that they have enjoyed throughout the course of their lives so far.

It is a book filled with inspiration, encouragement, wisdom and knowledge with the single intention of sharing the joy of the journey of empowerment with its readers.

Every woman's success shall serve as an inspiration to the reader, be they men, women, girls or boys alike. We are all at our strongest when we encourage each other, and it is a known fact that success is never achieved alone. Wisdom is the reward of experience, and its interpretation should always be shared.

Ever since humanity's cognitive awakening, people have shared their life-stories with each other, and their experiences have been passed on through generations. Think about cave paintings, campfire stories along many other examples within different cultures, of how life experiences have always been passed on through time. Even today, we enjoy sitting together with business partners or friends, exchanging, encouraging, and embracing stories.
As emotional learners, humans usually learn best when learning something from others. It is my intention to leave a positive impact on this world with these influential stories, that will surely leave traces of authentic inspiration on its readers.

Let true role models of Oman share their road to success with you. Be assured that diverse issues are the same all over this world- it does not matter where you live, what your background is, or who you are. This is particularly true for women given their diverse roles in life.

Personally, I have always loved learning from the world around me, especially from people with different backgrounds, cultures and countries. I have spent most of my career studying and working internationally, yet Oman quickly became my favourite place to go. This truly beautiful country has both fascinated educated me, as well as having had offered me the opportunity to meet numerous astonishing personalities. It was this fascination that motivated me to interview Omani women, and to let them share their exciting life-stories and individual insights with the world.

This book is written for all those who value and cherish one another's life experiences, those who are striving for success on their career path, for students aiming high and hungry to learn early, or even for people simply visiting Oman who are looking for a deeper understanding of the female culture.

Thus, Enjoy the winning strategies of these highly successful women sharing their inspiration, wisdom and encouragement through a huge bouquet of tips and tricks that may also lead you to become EMPOWERED!

September 2021

Ps.: I also hope you find joy in the beautiful pictures of Oman inside of this book; perhaps you have not yet visited this beautiful country, it may just be the inspiration you need to change that one day.

This book was written, with the intention of sharing the insights of 100 Successful Omani Women.

Although the author would have loved to have been able to conduct these interviews personally, Covid 19 and the lifestyle changes it has brought with it, sadly made it impossible for this to happen. Thus, the interviews were all carried out online.

The Omani Women who have participated in this project, were personally chosen by the author after extensive research and personal recommendations. All of the women were chosen from a variety of different backgrounds and have experienced numerous different paths that have led them to the successful lives that they are leading today.

Each contribution made to this book has enriched its content. The author feels very humbled and honoured to have contributions from some very well-known Omani role models who are already widely recognized for their success stories not only in Oman and The Middle East but also globally.

The interviews are made up from a selection of questions chosen individually by the Omani Women from a total of 20 questions. Each individual was able to choose which questions she answered and these were then summarized by the author. The summaries have been written in order to maintain the original wording and intention and every interview was approved by its contributor. Only the author had access to the conducted interviews.

The women represented in this book have been assembled in alphabetical order and all women have been referred to by their first names in order to ensure that neither hierarchy nor ranking had any influence on the content of the book. The author tried her very best to offer her readers a wide variety of stories, to enrich the books content. However, she is also very aware that she has by no means covered all successful women in Oman, this would have been an impossible task within the time limits.

Enjoy these inspiring stories.

Kathleen Nejad

The Sultanate of Oman, located on the Arabian Peninsula is an emerging international tourism destination in the Middle East.

The country has a population of around 4,5 million and around 40% of the population is female. Omani women have always been seen as essential contributors to the formation of the Omani society and they have continuously been empowered to take part in the development of the prosperity of Oman.

Omani women are typically seen as being passionate and dedicated to their work and they are recognised as equals by the Basic Law of the State.

Women have earned their place in society, be it in the private or public sector as well as in government institutions.

Over the past 50 years within the renaissance era in Oman, women have had unlimited access to education, training, and work. The late Majesty Sultan Qaboos Bin Said, instituted the legacy of empowerment of women in recognition for their leading role and their remarkable achievements. There are numerous success stories of Omani women some of which can be found within the pages of this unique book.

The world is full of empowering human beings and this book focuses on 100 Omani women who belong to this global group. It would have been near to impossible to have included the life story of every empowering woman in Oman, there were quite simply not enough pages available. The author would still like to acknowledge and thank every single one of those inspiring Omani women who all individually and collectively are helping to form a brighter world for the future of our children.

Enjoy this portable life coach – read the winning strategies of these highly successful Omani women and find your own journey to success!

*40%
female population

*4,5
million people

Suad Al Lamki (in memory of)

The late Suad Al Lamki inspired women of many generations throughout Oman and the Middle East. I am very thankful to her family, who provided me with the following information about her private life. I do have their permission to use and publish her details in this book. Thank you for your trust. Suad Al Lamki will continue to be a role model for others!

Role model
Suad grew up in a big family; she was the ninth child amongst seventeen brothers and sisters. Her father believed in the importance of the pursuit of knowledge. He offered all of his children equal opportunities to pursue their higher education at highly recognised universities and worked very hard to finance his children's studies. Her father was, most certainly, a source of inspiration and role model for Suad and her siblings.

Finding her passion
Ever since her childhood, Suad always had a fascination with the legal system. For instance, she always liked to read crime novels and watch movies with different investigational law scenes. These movies reflected the reality of courts—where accusations and claims of prosecution from one side are being raised, and from the other side, the defence and appeals from defence lawyers are presented. Seeing how cases were resolved and the type of skills, abilities

and personal characteristics that it takes to stand in the court hall was like finding and confirming her long-awaited passion. In a later stage of her life, one can even say that her passion for the law became an adored love.

Getting out of the comfort zone

At the age of ten, in Zanzibar, where she was born and raised, her father enrolled her in St. Joseph Convent school, a highly prestigious private school. After that, she went to Cairo to complete her secondary studies at the American College for Girls, now known as "Ramses College for Girls". She was then sent to Dublin for higher education, where she joined Trinity College in 1959 to study law. In 1962, Suad graduated and decided to join the "Honourable Society of King's Inns", the only society in Dublin that falls under the umbrella of Inns of Court.

There she was called to the Bar, after receiving the degree of Barrister-at-Law, in 1963. Lawyers holding this degree are the only lawyers permitted to practice as judges, public prosecutors, and defence lawyers in Dublin, England and Wales. Back then, it was not common for females to study law, not only in Ireland but rather in most of the European countries. Living in a sisters' dormitory that is known for its discipline and strictness probably also influenced her to become very disciplined throughout her life—indeed another reason for her success.

Finding solutions

In her batch, Suad Al Lamki was the only female studying law amongst all male students. In the beginning, this was uncomfortable and sometimes conflicting with the eastern cultural background many females grew up in at that time. Suad would not have been Suad without having a solution; she overcame these challenges by considering her male classmates as her brothers.

Her study time in Ireland coincided with the time of her other two brothers' studies. This meant a huge investment that had to be allocated and provided by their father to fund their studies. To ease the financial burden off their father's shoulders and secure some money for their living expenses, Suad and her brothers opted to stay and work in Ireland during the summer holidays. She always made the best out of her situations! A true lesson to learn.

Broaden your horizon

In addition to learning information, Suad believed in skills development that would be useful in her career as a lawyer. Thus, she joined various associations and societies, like the Elizabethan Society, a society that was engaging in activities such as discussion, debate, and application of principles. These activities were aimed at promoting higher-order thinking, such as critical thinking, analysis.

With her self-confidence, intelligence, sound debating skills, etc., she was a top-rated member of society. This attracted and encouraged many to invite her to join as key members of their societies.

Suad Al Lamki (in memory of)

Even though this meant adding more duties to her plate, seeing the power of networking that these societies will bring in, she accepted invitations. Hence, Suad became the chairperson's assistant of the Islamic society. Moreover, she was an active member in her capacity as the social secretary of the Union of Arab Students. This widened her horizon and enabled her to build many friendships with people from different cultures, nationalities, and specialisations. All this brought her a high amount of knowledge, experiences, and wealthy thoughts.

For Suad, keeping oneself productive and well informed were ongoing processes that never end. Thus, she continued seeking knowledge and never stopped working till the last days of her life. What a worrier she was!

Gaining extended work experiences

What Suad loved about her work was that she could implement it all: her education, her experiences and gained knowledge and her logical thinking. Working in law, you work on submitting clear proof and evidence that unveils the truth.

Good preparation is needed, supported by sound analytical skills, wisdom, and rational evidence. Furthermore, it is essential to convince officials in the court and/or people. Suad had it all; with her wisdom, charisma, skills and extensive experience, she rarely came out of a situation with an unfavourable outcome. For that, she not only earned women's respect but men's too.

Suad worked in different areas throughout her career; in courts as a public prosecutor and judge, lecturer, and as a legal advisor for multi-million dollars companies, and later in the Ministry of Legal Affairs where she presented the Government of Sultanate of Oman in negotiations such as Free Trade Agreement with the United States of America, renewal of concession agreement with Shell. She was always conscious, firm, and shared her profound values and knowledge.

She once said:

"Achieving righteousness is harder than defeating delusions."

100 Successful
Omani Women

Adila Al Ismaili

What was the best piece of advice that you were given regarding your career and that you will never forget?
Venture outside of your comfort zone!

What has shaped you the most in your life? Is there any specific situation?
Feeling responsible after losing my mother, may her soul rest in peace.

On the path to where you are now, what was the most determining step?
A decision to move from government to private companies.

Who would you identify as your role model? Whom do you look up to and why?
Her Excellency, the former Honourable Nashat Al Kharusi, started as an engineer in the telecom sector to reach the CEO of Telecommunications Regulatory Authority in Oman and was appointed into the state council. I admire her character, her adaptability, integrity, and courage.

What do you respect most in other successful women?
Intelligence, full-filling one position, passion, faith, adaptability, and courage.

What would you recommend to a student just starting and dreaming of a successful career?
To study in the field of where you want to work in the future and always to be passionate about learning.

If the entire world listened to you for five minutes, what would you say or what would you want to talk about?
If a woman is also a mother, I would say that she needs to balance both her successful career and, most importantly, her family to be able to enjoy her success.

What essential qualifications do you think will be needed ten years from now?
Technology, information, health, and energy & gas.

How would you describe your leadership style? What is your leadership motivation?
It is the mix of authoritarian & participative leadership, which allows me to learn more and increase my knowledge.

If there is a lot of work and you are under stress, how do you compensate?
Often, the stress of a deadline will motivate me to prioritise and organise the work to meet those due dates.

What are the three things in life you are most proud of?
I'm proud of myself and of how I created and fulfilled my dream. Furthermore, I thank my husband and boys for their support and understanding.

Group Financial Controller / Gulf Energy LLC- Gulf Energy SAOC
Board Member in Haya Water "Government company"

Do you do anything to keep you fit physically or mentally, and how often?
Walking five days a week, controlling what I eat, not increasing weight.

Which topics should humanity focus more on in the future?
I think crisis management, creative thinking, and digital skills.

What does it take to be a successful woman these days? What are the three top things successful business people should personalise?
Women need to have deep knowledge, be confident, focused, have courage and use networking. In my opinion, a top thing for businesspeople should be to be fearless, understand finance, and grow as a leader.

Is there a quote you favour that suits you? Or an important book you read that influenced you?
Success is a state of mind. If you want to succeed - start thinking of yourself as being successful (by Dr Joyce Brothers).

If you had extra time of four hours a day, what would you do during that time?
Spend more time with my family and read more about new things around us.

What are your most important goals? Is there a difference for you between life goals and career goals?
I am satisfied that I reached my career goal, to be CFO, through very hard work.
Now, I'm keen on passing all my knowledge to my team and my colleagues.

What is your favourite place in Oman, that you like to visit in order to relax and recharge your batteries?
Mirbat in Dhofar.

Ahlam Hamoud Al Jahwari

What was the best piece of advice that you were given regarding your career and that you will never forget?
Work silently! The best advice I could give to another is to let your work speak for you, and it will do you justice.

On the path to where you are now, what was the most determining step?
I can take a critical decision and take responsibility for that decision. The decisive step in my life was the courageous decision I took on a rainy December 2003 to change the college to the one I wanted from the start. From that moment, I truly liked what I did, and I was very successful in my career.

Who would you identify as your role model? Whom do you look up to and why?
I believe I am the harvest of the people I've dealt with, the experiences I've had, and the words that have touched my soul and mind. "We owe all those who pass through the clocks of our days, and we owe more to those who have not yet crossed!" But I owe it to my mother and father because they reflect everything beautiful that I believe in and strive for. And because life in its separate ways needs a companion, my husband is that companion on my journey.

What would you recommend to a student just starting and dreaming of a successful career?
My advice is, "Follow your passion!" Do what you want, what you strongly desire, and what really expresses your faith and translates your capabilities. So, be what you want, not what others want! You will be happy because happiness is not the moment of reaching the goal of turning the dream into reality, but rather the path leading to the ultimate moment, and you have to start another dream!

If the entire world listened to you for five minutes, what would you say or what would you want to talk about?
We are all on a journey on one ship towards happiness. Let this journey and this world be safe by spreading the values of love, tolerance, and justice rising above hate, hatred, and injustice. History is a court and will judge us according to what will remain in the memory. As the German historian Friedrich Schiller said, "The history of the world is the court of the world!"

What are the three things in life you are most proud of?
The things I am most proud of in my life: first, my principles that I do not give up, "He lives

without honour who lives without principles!" The important thing is not to reach the goal but to achieve it in a way that expresses my principles! Second, forming a lovely family with three children. The family achieves inner peace and security for the person and pushes to unlimited giving. Third, my free and responsible choices and my defence of them.

What does it take to be a successful woman these days? What are the three top things successful business people should personalise?
A woman will be successful when she truly believes in herself. Additionally, it is vital to have the support of the family and to create opportunities and possibilities.

What would you devote your time and energy to if you were to invest now, in your future best self?
For me, "time" is the most precious thing I have, and I can trade money for time to get time! So, therefore, I will put my time and energy into writing and research production because that embodies what I believe in.

Is there a quote you favour that suits you? Or an important book you read that influenced you?
A quote I love is, "I believe that history is court, and we are just pending cases that swing between memory or oblivion!". And since talking about quotes, I can't go beyond the words stuck in my memory that sharpen my enthusiasm when it fades, as the Algerian novelist Ahlam Mosteghanemi said, "Dreams are created to come true." I was also greatly influenced by the Egyptian writer Farouk Gweideh, "Our dreams are still in the mud that we plant. If life goes away, the dream is not deported."

What are your most important goals? Is there a difference for you between life goals and career goals?
Life without purpose means slow death! Therefore, our existence in life has a purpose and a goal that we should realise and direct all our energy to achieve, and all our temporary goals related to family or job should push us to that. Generally, our professional goals are momentary and circumstantial. However, our goals in life are permanent as long as we live, and here I remember the words of the American writer Robert Schuller, "Goals are not only necessary to motivate us but are essential to our survival." In short, my goal is to leave something useful for humanity.

How would you describe yourself in three words? Do you live with a daily routine, and what is your secret to success?
I live on an organised day and not on a daily routine. I cannot imagine tomorrow without having a plan for it, which is not in any way harmful or an obstacle to enjoying life; but in an organised manner that brings me production and something useful. I would describe myself in three words: I dream, I plan, I execute. What makes me successful is my desire to do so and employ my skills in the right direction. The French philosopher Rene Descartes said, "I think, therefore I am," and I say, "I dream, therefore I am."

Ahlam Jahdhami

What was the best piece of advice that you were given regarding your career and that you will never forget?
I got so much great advice, and I still do, partially because I seek it. The advice that shaped my career path was my first week at a job where I almost quit. I worked in the hot desert, wearing a coverall soaked by mud on an oil rig platform. My face showed defeat and an inability to withstand the harshness of this environment. A colleague, an older gentleman, approached me with assertiveness and determination, telling me I can only limit myself, and nothing could break me unless I allow it to; if I'm to believe I am weak, then I am!

What has shaped you the most in your life? Is there any specific situation?
The long, sleepless hours operating in hostile environments in remote places made me feel I could survive any situation in life. There is nothing that can physically wear me down. Funny enough, it prepared me for motherhood.

On the path to where you are now, what was the most determining step?
I remained in this line of business despite the setbacks and because of them. I knew by enduring the challenges; I was paving the path for younger female engineers, which gave me a sense of gratification and purpose.

Who would you identify as your role model? Whom do you look up to and why?
I believe having one person to look up to would be limiting. I'm lucky to be surrounded by many souls that inspire me. My grandma is the ultimate idol. She had no formal education, couldn't read or write, yet single-handedly raised a large family. She emits strength in will, resilience, and persistence, is very adaptive to life's continuous changes and entirely at peace with what's to come. She recently asked me to download a game on her smartphone as she's fascinated by how the younger generation spends hours staring at their phone playing! I never did.

What do you respect most in other successful women?
I am blessed to be surrounded by women who continuously amaze me and inspire me, my daughter, and even my son. Some characteristics that stand out to me are integrity, empowering others, a strong code of ethics, intelligence, paving a path in their respective careers, enabling younger female coworkers to walk through, success not run by ego, humbleness, and most of all, kindness.

What would you recommend to a student just starting and dreaming of a successful career?
The monotony of any job can hinder progress: finding passion in minor things and keeping one's awareness aligned to that passion helps the mind stay focused.

Sales Marketing Manager / Special Oilfield Services CO. L.L.C.

If the entire world listened to you for five minutes, what would you say or what would you want to talk about?
Men and women need to be treated just. To me, the noun 'Feminist' is a synonym for a humanist:
a core belief that humankind's welfare and dignity are integral, irrespective of gender.

What essential qualifications do you think will be needed ten years from now?
Confidence, emotional intelligence, integrity and perhaps a college degree.

If there is a lot of work and you are under stress, how do you compensate?
Meditation is an excellent form of introspection. Whenever stress escalates, I channel the stress
through various activities so I achieve physical wellbeing.

What are the three things in life you are most proud of?
My children, my children & my children. Motherhood has been one of my favourite roles in life, and I
adore being present in it.

Do you do anything to keep you fit physically or mentally, and how often?
At the age of three, my son looked up at me and said lovingly, 'You look as beautiful as a cow'
(and yes, he's still alive).

After two children, I felt physically unwell,
so I decided to heal it and remain active. I
pick up different hobbies to avoid boredom
and monotony. I walk regularly; I dive occasionally; I hike often, and I practice yoga. I'm
planning on cycling again. I also go through
periods of static mode where I do nothing,
and I've learned to allow myself to do that,
then I pick up where I left and repeat.

**Which topics should humanity focus more
on in the future?**
Mindfulness. We go through life gaining
knowledge about various outward matters
with a continuous bombardment of detailed
information, but we should focus more on
one's inner self.

Aisha Al Saifi

What was the best piece of advice that you were given regarding your career and that you will never forget?
My mom always reminded me that the best way of living a life of choice for a woman is to be financially independent. So she made sure that my sisters and I pursued our education and were all leading economically independent lives.

What has shaped you the most in your life? Is there any specific situation?
I was always determined to innovate my way of life. In my last 15 years of being an active Omani poet, I went through different battles to acquire the freedom to express myself and navigate social, religious, and cultural dilemmas. First, I was a poet who anonymously published poems behind an alias. Then I became a poet who writes with her real name and shows up publicly. My third development is that I am now writing freely about all kinds of different subjects. Finally, I discovered all of it was 100% worth it, and I saw the fruits of these battles.

What essential qualifications do you think will be needed ten years from now?
Resilience as we live in a rapidly changing world. Agility, as the world connects more and more. Cultural Openness: to innovate our ways, lives, families and careers through diverse cultures and communities. For example, where people become the centre of attention, and our ability to connect with others becomes key to developing and growing professionally and personally.

How would you describe your leadership style? What is your leadership motivation?
I don't follow a specific leadership style, but instead, I adopt situational leadership dictated to the context and people. The approach I follow differs based on the person's knowledge, confidence, and willingness to contribute. Usually, I dedicate time to understanding my team's spirit and work dynamics. What motivates each member is unique and how to get the best of them is through making them feel empowered. The sources of empowerment for each is what shifts the equation by unlocking their maximum potential.

If there is a lot of work and you are under stress, how do you compensate?
Leading different roles in life; a poet, engineer, wife, daughter, and mother; each with significant responsibilities, has left its toll on my wellbeing at certain times. I have different ways

Director Market Intelligence / ASYAD Group

---

of managing stress based on its level, its source, and the luxury of time I have. (I take a long drive with some classical music played loud, or sometimes a very thoughtful shower or frankincense would freshen up my night). On the days when I felt completely burnt out, I would escape to a motel. Sometimes a massive workout session would end up making me feel renewed again. I also like hiking and diving as it has a great connection with the earth. You then see the smallest details of the beauty of this planet. Finally, writing has always been a significant escape.

What are the three things in life you are most proud of?
My roots (a village girl who has travelled the world but never forgot her humble beginnings), my poetry and its messages (to reflect the voiceless and the unheard voices behind the veil). I am supporting other women in need, be it financially, career-wise or even emotionally.

Do you do anything to keep you fit physically or mentally, and how often?
I never felt the need to exercise until April 2020, where I started to feel depressed because of a lack of mobility during the COVID-19 lockdowns. My body was exhausted, as well as my mind. I then decided to invest 10% of my income into my fitness and hired a personal trainer. Since then, I have made a shift in my fitness journey and my life and nutrition choices. I now exercise three times a week and follow a diet plan. I also started diving, and I would either hike or dive during the weekend.

What are your most important goals? Is there a difference for you between life goals and career goals?
If you asked me this question two years ago, my answer would have been completely different. I would answer, I want to become a CEO in my thirties, work in X number of countries and deliver X number of millions' worth of projects. During COVID-19, I had a deep reflection and re-prioritization of life. I now dream of a happy,profound, and meaningful life with my loved ones. I want to live to write beautiful poetry that can capture my diverse mix of feelings and re-create my life and others' lives in a creative, artistic way. I look to become closer to my inner soul. My career goals used to dictate my life goals, but I'm at that stage where I have aligned my career goals to serve the bigger vision in life.

Did the Omani culture you grew up in have an impact on your career path?
It did indeed. Being a daughter and granddaughter to inspiring and strong women, who despite their restricted upbringings, believed in my mission, poetry and career, makes me more determined to take my message further. Moreover, as embraced by the Omani culture, the humbleness gave me a sense of ease to connect with people from all cultures and age groups.

What is your favourite place in Oman, that you like to visit in order to relax and recharge your batteries?
Since the lockdown, I started roaming around where I found plenty of what I call 'my secret runaways', virgin beaches, mountainous spots, isolated hills, and quiet villages on the outskirts of Muscat.

Alena Dique

What was the best piece of advice that you were given regarding your career and that you will never forget?
There is a great deal to learn when it comes to pursuing and excelling in your career. As you continue developing, you will probably come in contact with many pieces of career advice. When I started my career, the best advice was, "View every person you meet as a door that may lead you to a new opportunity". You never know how a person can add to your life professionally or personally if you don't give them a chance.

What has shaped you the most in your life? Is there any specific situation?
When I think of things that made me the person I am today, I can say that my family played a huge part. Sometimes, you don't realise how much of an impact family has, whether parents, siblings, aunts, uncles, cousins, etc. Life is constantly changing; however, the family will continue to stand firm and support you with their best, so you can be your best.

Who would you identify as your role model? Whom do you look up to and why?
I don't think it's fair to mention just one role model. However, I admire and stay motivated, learning from the lives of many hard-working, passionate individuals. I respect these traits in Angela Merkel, Mother Teresa, Anne Frank, Anna Wintour, APJ Abdul Kalam, Late Sultan Qaboos bin Said and aspired to emulate them in my own life.

What do you respect most in other successful women?
In terms of the corporate world, successful women don't dream about being the best in their field, they decide to be the best in their state or country, and most want to change the world if the opportunity presents itself. They are undeniably ambitious, grateful for their success, and choose their battles wisely. Women, in general, are super-beings; they possess qualities of persistence, poise and passion in all things they do.

What would you recommend to a student just starting and dreaming of a successful career?
Do your best to show up early and be ready to complete your assigned tasks. Each job you will have is essential for building your career and character. Employers will appreciate and notice your effort, and you will continue to stay on good terms if you display your eagerness in your work.

How would you describe your leadership style? What is your leadership motivation?
Definitely, collaborative leadership style. Moving from the top down to the team-centric format to create an inclusive environment that energises teams, releases creativity, and cultivates a work culture that is both productive and joyful. I learned of this collective intelligence approach during my training at the United Nations Conference on Trade and Development (UNCTAD) in Geneva, Switzerland.

Which topics should humanity focus more on in the future?
Lifelong Learning: You can continue to learn no matter what age or stage of your career you

Business Consultant - SME Development | Corporate and Youth Trainer – Ministry of Higher Education, Research, and Innovation

are in. Possessing a willingness to learn is an attribute that is highly valued in today's workforce. Asking the crucial questions: Many successful professionals have become successful because they ask important questions. Therefore, you should maintain a curious disposition and ask questions.

What does it take to be a successful woman these days? What are the three top things successful business people should personalise?
It is vital to set realistic goals - Setting goals will help keep you motivated throughout your career. You should set periodic achievable goals and reward yourself when you meet the goals you set. This will help you build confidence, and most often, you will find that you can do the things you thought you could not do. The three things successful business people should personalise would be company culture, personal priorities and a self-care routine.

Is there a quote you favour that suits you? Or an important book you read that influenced you?
"Be confident, yet humble." Confidence can lead to productivity at work. Therefore, it is vital to develop your confidence to communicate your ideas in any situation effectively. However, remain humble, and always accept that you will not always be the one who knows the most.

Do you do anything to keep you fit physically or mentally, and how often?
Mental fitness is very crucial. My mantra is 'Minimise Noise and Maximise Motivation'. Shut out the constant stream of negative thoughts that run through your mind. That mental static is your biggest obstacle. Learning to filter it by concentrating on positive thinking is crucial to your success. To do this, you must be completely clear concerning your conscious self. Similarly, a lasting motivation can't start from an outside source; it must come from a personal, ingrained need for change and development.

What is your favourite place in Oman, that you like to visit in order to relax and recharge your batteries?
That's a difficult one, especially since I've lived in Oman all my life; there are too many. However, I have lovely memories of boating at the Qantab beach, day trips to Nakhal, driving down Muttrah corniche when it's drizzling and exploring Salalah during the Khareef season.

Alia Al Qalam Al Yafie

Who would you identify as your role model? Whom do you look up to and why?
My late father, as a man of sound principles. He convinced me I could work in such a
male-dominated environment as aviation, which eventually made me become the first female
aircraft engineer in the Gulf. I recall when I chose to study aviation, my father, who was
my greatest supporter, said: "You have to be responsible for your choice, and you can't stop
halfway through and say I can't make it." This phrase, until today, motivates me.

What do you respect most in other successful women?
I admire the most about successful women: the determination to work hard to make a change, the amount of creativity they possess, and all the effort they put into their success. They have an advanced perspective towards different matters and bring value into what they do. Seeing successful women unite brings joy to me.

What would you recommend to a student just starting and dreaming of a successful career?
I recommend discovering the true passion and pursuing it. Always put your total capacity in achieving and always try to do the ultimate best. Yes, it might initially be difficult, but all hard work pays off in the end, and when you accomplish all achievements, you will genuinely be proud and fulfilled of how far you came.

If the entire world listened to you for five minutes, what would you say or what would you want to talk about?
I would state that everyone deserves a chance to prove themselves regardless of their identity trait. I believe equal opportunities should be given, as anyone with high capabilities should have the opportunity to prove themselves.

How would you describe your leadership style? What is your leadership motivation?
I would say that I have a direct leadership style; I enjoy working with my team and delegate

tasks to them so everything goes efficiently. We always try to achieve a specific target within a period and try to evolve. I would say that I have a strategic mind when it comes to leading and a vision that comes in handy while working.

What are the three things in life you are most proud of?
I'd say being a mother to 4 amazing children and a wife to a loving and supporting husband, and being a skilled expert in my field. I'm proud of myself for reaching that far and succeeding in what I do!

What does it take to be a successful woman these days? What are the three top things successful business people should personalise?
I say you need to be fearless and daring to succeed, and decision-making would be an essential factor, too. You should be confident in the choices you make to reach the top. I would also add, with the help of family, you will flourish and excel in what you do.

Is there a quote you favour that suits you? Or an important book you read that influenced you?
I'm currently reading a book called "Principles" by Ray Dalio. This book is inspiring and extraordinary. Although it speaks about the ups and downs of success and how sometimes it's difficult to attain it, it also demonstrates how technology is vital for innovation and progress.

If you had extra time of four hours a day, what would you do during that time?
I'd watch more news since it's an essential part of my day. Coming from a family of politicians will cause you to want to learn more about the outside world.

What are your most important goals? Is there a difference for you between life goals and career goals?
My most important goal now is to take care of my kids and raise them to be the best. I always tell them that they're future leaders, as it's essential to be strong to live in this world, and it is important for them to believe in themselves and cause a change in the future.

How would you describe yourself in three words, and what is your secret to success?
Punctual, committed, passionate are three words I'd use to describe myself. But being full of determination and positivity also helped me reach where I am.

What is your favourite place in Oman, that you like to visit in order to relax and recharge your batteries?
I'm from the south. Being in my hometown Salalah makes me relax and calm.

Al Sayyida Basma Al Said

What was the best piece of advice that you were given regarding your career and that you will never forget?
One of the most important is "appreciate your work and build on it". Just build on what you have and don't always feel like you have to do more and more. Also, don't take work home.

What has shaped you the most in your life? Is there any specific situation?
What shaped me is any failure that I've gone through, whether work or personal life. Learning how to do it right when you fail is a big success. You then learn, update yourself, and gain new knowledge.

On the path to where you are now, what was the most determining step?
The most decisive step was me leaving the government and opening the first mental health clinic in Oman. I felt I needed to open a clinic. It's been a dream that I've wanted since I graduated. So although I had a secured job, I took that big step in my life as I did not want to miss the challenge as a chance.

If the entire world listened to you for five minutes, what would you say or what would you want to talk about?
I would talk about passion, passion in everything you do and living the moment. I think these two things are what I'd be talking about because lots of other things would come out through that. So, yes, passion and living the moment.

What essential qualifications do you think will be needed ten years from now?
Many would say it's qualifications or certificates. But, for me, it is hands-on training, learning in different places, and keeping on learning from life.
Travelling, for instance, means meeting people and establishing significant new connections. Helping people and humanity - doing something good for the world besides your work should also be necessary.

How would you describe your leadership style? What is your leadership motivation?
My leadership style has always been teamwork and learning from everyone. In my opinion, that's strong leadership, including different ideas. Without cooperation, you don't succeed; you can't do it all alone.

**Mental Health Specialist & Owner / Whispers of Serenity Clinic
Founder / Not Alone Mental Health Campaign Oman**

If there is a lot of work and you are under stress, how do you compensate?
Throughout the years, it changed. Music and arts always helped. I love decorating and being creative
with themes for gatherings. To destress, I enjoy decorating, listening to music and sitting with people
who make me laugh.

What are the three things in life you are most proud of?
I'm proud of being a mom and able to balance family, work, myself and relationships. I am also proud
of being a good daughter. And finally, I am very proud of my clinic and my work. We help many
people, society and even the world, as we are spreading the importance of mental health awareness
internationally. Finally, I'm proud of myself for not giving up, pushing it through and loving every
moment.

Which topics should humanity focus more on in the future?
Teaching people how to have passion and accepting themselves is so important. Mental health is a
topic that needs more focus. Especially, the youth should learn to put themselves forward and to be
mindful. It is vital that you know how to cope when it comes to your mental health.

What does it take to be a successful woman these days? What are the three top things successful
business people should personalise?
I think men and women are going through the same things. We're an army of women. We need to
fight for equality, move, work, and we need to build on what we have. Women need to collaborate and
be innovative and creative. We see throughout history the strength of women once they decide to do
things right.

Is there a quote you favour that suits you? Or an important book you read that influenced you?
My motto is that the change begins with you. I think you have a choice in your life. Even if you're
in a cage, you have an option to continue living or giving up, for example. One of the books I like,
which is easy to read, is called "Don't Sweat the Small Stuff".

It shows you simple ways to keep the little things from overtaking your life. Start working on yourself
and make that change. It's your choice to want to make that tremendous change.

How would you describe yourself in three words? Do you live with a daily routine, and what is
your secret to success?
I'm not too fond of routine, so I don't have a set way or system. When it comes to working, it's a
bit different. However, I do sessions inside my office; sometimes, I walk on the beach with a client,
sometimes we do art and talk about mental health, etc. I feel the routine kills the excitement. So,
I always try not to. I'm learning every day till I die. I describe myself as spontaneous, creative and I
love doing things outside of the box.

Al Sayyida Mayya Al Said

What was the best piece of advice that you were given regarding your career and that you will never forget?
As a violinist, my teacher would say, "Practice makes perfect". I took that advice and translated it into the other positions I have filled within my career by constantly learning and always trying new things and applying them. If something doesn't work out the first time, keep on trying until it does.

On the path to where you are now, what was the most determining step?
Taking the risk of leaving my job and going all in doing what I am most passionate about, which is coaching. Coaching divorced women rebuild their lives.

Who would you identify as your role model? Whom do you look up to and why?
I find inspiration in everyone's story; there is not ONE person who I look up to. However, I believe everyone who overcomes an obstacle, dedicates and commits to their goal is someone to look up to.

What do you respect most in other successful women?
They are a force to be reckoned with; they don't give up or make excuses; they get things done! These women continue to reach their goals, and once they do, they set an example for others. What I respect even more is seeing them help others on their way up.

What would you recommend to a student just starting and dreaming of a successful career?
To know that any path they choose, they will face setbacks/challenges along. That it is ok, and it is all part of the journey. Focus on enjoying and taking care of their mental health and not being so hard on themselves. To be loving, gentle and supportive when speaking to themselves to believe that they can do it!

If the entire world listened to you for five minutes, what would you say or what would you want to talk about?
I want to remind the world that we MUST find a way to share the earth we live on peacefully and respectfully despite our differences. We are in this together, and we must support one another as much as we can. Our life and our futures depend on it.

How would you describe your leadership style? What is your leadership motivation?
To lead by example and with integrity. To be authentic when delivering my talks and to speak from the heart. If there is one thing that I want to communicate with my audience or team is relatability.

If there is a lot of work and you are under stress, how do you compensate?
I am taking a mini-break from it all by working out, journaling with a cup of tea, or helping someone else.

Coach | Speaker | Content Creator

Do you do anything to keep you fit physically or mentally, and how often?
Physically, I work out approximately 4-5 days a week and mentally journal when I need to.

What does it take to be a successful woman these days? What are the three top things successful business people should personalise?
The decision to want to be a successful person. Have a message, find a niche and work hard to make a change. Be clear on what success means to you.

Is there a quote you favour that suits you? Or an important book you read that influenced you?
"Grow through what you go through" is one of my favourites.

If you had extra time of four hours a day, what would you do during that time?
I would spend it with my family.

What are your most important goals? Is there a difference for you between life goals and career goals?
I feel that the goals should be aligned, one should have a purpose in life and that all plans should contribute to the purpose. My goal is to help women discover their potential and support them in living a life they love.

How would you describe yourself in three words? Do you live with a daily routine, and what is your secret to success?
I value time, so I usually have everything that I need to do listed, and I follow as much as I can. I describe myself as committed, hardworking, and intentional. Being authentic is a huge part of my success.

What is your favourite place in Oman, that you like to visit in order to relax and recharge your batteries?
Oman has a lot to offer. I can't just pick one place; however, I generally love exploring and discovering Oman's beautiful nature. Hikes in Jabal Akhdar, visiting the villages, being out at sea. Being out in nature allows me to recharge, relax and recover.

Amal Al Raisi

What has shaped you the most in your life? Is there any specific situation?
The challenges I faced initially while starting up my brand opened up my mind and thought process. It made me realise that I will continue to face challenges in life, but I should consistently push myself to set the bar higher after each phase of my business.

On the path to where you are now, what was the most determining step?
I discovered my passion for fashion while I was on the hunt for my wedding dress. When I couldn't find one that my heart desired, I decided to design my own. The process of creating my dress from start to finish and the accomplishment I felt wearing it on my wedding day was indescribable. This fuelled my passion and was the most defining moment in my career.

Who would you identify as your role model? Whom do you look up to and why?
Because of his faithfulness and commitment towards Oman, my dad inspires me every day to work as hard.

What do you respect most in other successful women?
Their hard work and determination to chase their dreams while being there for their families are what I truly respect for every one of them. It is a true testament to their success.

What would you recommend to a student just starting and dreaming of a successful career?
I would advise them to follow their dreams and work hard to achieve what they truly believe in. A successful career doesn't come easy; it is a road filled with challenges. The key is to have faith, stay positive, and perceive every challenge as a lesson towards growth.

How would you describe your leadership style? What is your leadership motivation?
I believe in an open management system; teamwork as a robust and supportive team is the key to the success of any brand. Working hand-in-hand and allowing my team to voice their ideas helps build a better business.

What are the three things in life you are most proud of?
My family, my passion towards my brand and supporting local Omani talent. Oman is filled with an abundance of talent and skills that need to be showcased to the rest of the world. As a proud Omani, I strive hard to do just this as a way of giving back to the country that has provided us with endless opportunities.

Do you do anything to keep you fit physically or mentally, and how often?
Since the pandemic, I have been trying to dedicate some time to work out whenever possible. This helps me to stay positive and lead a healthy lifestyle.

Owner & Creative Director / Amal AL Raisi Fashion House

Is there a quote you favour that suits you? Or an important book you read that influenced you?
"Dreams don't work unless we do" is a quote that I live by. A simple yet straightforward quote that keeps me motivated to achieve my goals. Atomic Habits by James Clear is a book that has inspired me to take charge of every day.

How would you describe yourself in three words? Do you live with a daily routine, and what is your secret to success?
I have a daily routine that ensures that I get time to spend with my family and take care of the brand. I would describe myself as passionate, dedicated, and caring. Learning from my mistakes and taking every challenge as a lesson in disguise is what has brought me to where I am today.

Did the Omani culture you grew up in have an impact on your career path?
Definitely! The Omani culture, traditions and history are deeply embedded in my brand. I like to incorporate a piece of Omani heritage in my designs to showcase Omani talent and craftsmanship and its story to the world. Drawing inspiration from the beauty around Oman, such as Al Baleed, the UNESCO World Heritage Site or Musandam's beautiful Khors and dramatic mountains, I try to translate elements from here through signature embroidery and silhouettes encapsulating a piece of Oman.

What is your favourite place in Oman, that you like to visit in order to relax and recharge your batteries?
That would be Jabal Akhtar. Immersing myself in the beauty of nature makes it the perfect place to destress.

(Dr.) Amina Abdullah Al Balushi

What was the best piece of advice that you were given regarding your career and that you will never forget?
My colleague, Dr Ali Nasir, who, at the time, was the adviser in the Ministry of Tourism, encouraged me to continue my PhD studies in the field of tourism development. Tourism is one of the priority sectors in Oman's Vision 2040. Dr. Nasir specified that the country needs highly qualified Omanis to contribute to developing a sustainable tourism sector that meets the country's vision in diversifying the economy while taking care of the Omani heritage, culture and natural environment. So even though my journey in achieving my PhD was faced with some challenges, I immensely enjoyed my time at the University of Glasgow, which provided me with the determination.

What has shaped you the most in your life? Is there any specific situation?
Two key aspects shaped me throughout my life. First, and early on in life, I was blessed with three children and a supportive husband who shaped my life into what it is today, whereby I learned to become responsible and nurturing whilst balancing that with my own goals. Secondly, a significant part of my career is the work I conducted regarding developing the Oman Tourism National Strategy. The Strategy played a pivotal role in shaping me as well as developing my skills.

On the path to where you are now, what was the most determining step?
As an individual who would like to give back to Oman, I am currently on a path that entails contributing to the plans for the development of the local communities and maximising their benefits from tourism development whilst maintaining quality levels. The most decisive step was my decision to commence and achieve my PhD, which helped develop my knowledge in local community development.

What do you respect most in other successful women?
Being a successful woman, be it an entrepreneur or a housewife, means having the courage to own who you are and sustaining the values and morals that shape you. I especially respect women who have achieved the balance of responsibilities and perspective in all aspects of their lives.

Advisor of Research and Studies /
The Ministry of Heritage and Tourism

What would you recommend to a student just starting and dreaming of a successful career?
I would recommend the students to follow their instincts concerning choosing their field of expertise.
I would encourage students to venture outside of their comfort zones, to travel and experience other
cultures as such experiences help in adapting oneself whilst at the same time maintaining discipline
and work.

If the entire world listened to you for five minutes, what would you say or what would you want
to talk about?
I would say that life is too short; take risks, learn from your mistakes, and enjoy every aspect of it. Be
grateful and regret nothing, as I believe everything happens for a purpose, and you should seek that
purpose.

What essential qualifications do you think will be needed ten years from now?
An essential qualification will be technological innovation with commercial awareness. The adoption and use of technology will only grow from now on. Hence, an individual must adapt to such
technological changes, especially those relevant to one's career and field, as they could ease the way
commercial thinking, sense, and understanding occur.

How would you describe your leadership style? What is your leadership motivation?
Establishing roles and reporting lines in a team is essential. I tend to utilise a leadership style that entails teamwork between the leader and the team members as it allows the leader to guide and support
the team through sharing knowledge and expertise whilst at the same time measuring the outcomes
and advice to deliver the best results. Regarding leadership motivation, I usually am passionate about
my work and aim to achieve the best results. Hence, the realisation of said results will drive my
motivation to lead my team and their dedication to utilising the available resources within the given
timelines to deliver.

What are the three things in life you are most proud of?
I'm proud of being a mother of three successful young leaders. Also, I'm pleased with my career
development at the Ministry of Heritage and Tourism while having the opportunity to contribute to
Oman's tourism development.

What is your favourite place in Oman, that you like to visit in order to relax and recharge your
batteries?
We have diverse scenery and nature, hence to me, Oman is a paradise for relaxing; Musandam's
beaches and mountains, Dhofar's green mountains, Ad Dakhiliyah and its cultural and natural scener-
ies, Al Batinah's long beaches and cultural heritage, Al Wusta's white beaches. However, my favourite
remains to be Al Sharqiya and its Sands.

Areej Al Ismaili

What was the best piece of advice that you were given regarding your career and that you will never forget?
Take risks, explore new opportunities, get out of your comfort zone, and get involved in many areas that will ultimately serve a bigger purpose.

What has shaped you the most in your life? Is there any specific situation?
I wouldn't relate to a specific situation. I would say the values and principles instilled in me as a child have shaped my life. The two most important values were religion and family. Religion came first, no matter what, and this has always been my first step before I decided to do anything. Family values and traditions, which I realize day by day, are essential to maintaining healthy wellbeing, and it is also the main drive behind my career choices.

What do you respect most in other successful women?
I mostly respect their genuineness, integrity, and resilience.

What would you recommend to a student just starting and dreaming of a successful career?
Don't restrict your opportunities based on what the paper from your university says. On the contrary, it is always wise to remain open to new challenges and opportunities because that is where you will probably find your true passion.

If there is a lot of work and you are under stress, how do you compensate?
I try my best to always stop before I get stressed out because I know work will never end, and there is no point in exhausting myself because that will make me stop enjoying what I do. I've gone through work-related stress previously, and it was not worth the time I've taken away from the most important values in my life.

What are the three things in life you are most proud of?
I am proud of the family I come from and the family I am creating with my husband.
I am proud of my ability to face failures and take the time to reflect to do better.
I am proud as I strive towards my definition of success and not compare to how a "standard" success ladder looks like in the eyes of others.

Do you do anything to keep you fit physically or mentally, and how often?
On average, I walk four times a week. I go on early morning walks around the neighbourhood and by the beach. Breathing in the fresh air, listening to the birds tweeting and witnessing sunrise makes me happy and sets my day to a great start.

VP – Corporate Support Services / Tibiaan Properties

Which topics should humanity focus more on in the future?
Mental health, relationship skills and financial literacy. Is there a quote you favour that suits you? Or an important book you read that influenced you?

The Happiness Trap, by Russ Harris. This book focuses on creating a rich and meaningful life and has helped me cope with difficulties in my career and personal life.

If you had extra time of four hours a day, what would you do during that time?
An ideal answer to this question would probably be learning a new language or a new skill, but realistically, with a newborn, I would spend that time getting some more sleep!

Did the Omani culture you grew up in have an impact on your career path?
I grew up in a family where it was natural and expected from everyone to study and go to work, so it was already established that I would do that. I was raised by working parents who always encouraged us to work hard and become independent. Naturally, I was guided and advised, but I was never questioned about my career choices or forced into a specific direction.

What is your favourite place in Oman, that you like to visit in order to relax and recharge your batteries?
Oman is a beautiful country with so much to offer, and even though I don't have a specific favourite place, I can say that there is always a place to recharge, depending on what I feel like.

There is no particular rule about the beach being the relaxing spot, mountains, wadis, or desert. Sometimes, taking a stroll by the bustling and busy Souq Muttrah does the work for me!

Areej Mohsin Haider Darwish

Areej Mohsin Haider Darwish

Who would you identify as your role model? Whom do you look up to and why?
My role model will always be my father. He always motivated and encouraged me to strive to reach my true potential. His visionary thoughts and ideas, impeccable attention to detail, determination, and passion for his work were qualities of which I was in awe. The path to success is not a straight line. It's very often a curved one with challenges along the way. My father taught and motivated me to overcome them and often proved that no obstacle is big enough to overcome. He would boost my confidence and tell me, "If you aim higher than you expect, you could reach higher than you dreamed." His words of wisdom and guidance are something that I will always cherish.

What do you respect most in other successful women?
What I respect in any other successful woman is not only their achievements and how they have scaled to success but their passion, enthusiasm and the challenges they have overcome to reach the position they are in. I respect women for their inner strength, ingenuity, and, most importantly, how they balance their lives to make them more fulfilling.

What would you recommend to a student just starting and dreaming of a successful career?
Focus on your education. Grow your skills and knowledge and keep your skills updated. Set realistic goals to pursue your passion and stay focused. Achieving success takes time and is a lot of hard work. Strive for excellence, remain motivated and be determined to achieve your goals.

What essential qualifications do you think will be needed ten years from now?
Education plays a vital role. The world of work is evolving at a fast pace. There is every likelihood that the qualifications of today may not suffice for future roles. With the rise of technological innovation and digital technology, I foresee many opportunities for this field. Everyone worldwide depends on technology; being digitally literate and qualified in artificial intelligence, e-science, and emerging technologies would be a plus.

Though technology would be the sought after qualification, we cannot replace the human element completely. Analytical thinking, critical thinking and problem-solving skills will grow in prominence. Management qualification would continue to play a significant role as business management, human resource management, and financial management form the core of any business. As healthcare plays an essential role in our daily lives, demand for medical professionals would soar.

How would you describe your leadership style? What is your leadership motivation?
I have always believed in the participative leadership style. We build a vision, set clear goals and map a path for our team. It's important to encourage collaboration and keep the communication lines open. It facilitates a free flow of ideas & improves morale. Decision-making becomes a collective endeavour as it taps into the employee's skills, ideas, and potential. The employees will always enjoy working in an environment where their views and participation

Chairperson - ACERE / Mohsin Haider Darwish LLC

are respected. It challenges the employees to outdo themselves and work towards a common goal. Sharing our vision, long-term strategy and organizational goals have always motivated them and increased their productivity and creativity.

If there is a lot of work and you are under stress, how do you compensate?
Stress is inevitable at work, especially as we have to keep pace with the dynamic business environment. However, we can handle stress effectively by prioritizing and organizing tasks. I also strive to maintain a healthy work-life balance by taking regular breaks, which helps rejuvenate me.

What are the three things in life you are most proud of?
There are many things in my life for which I am truly grateful. The first which makes me proud is my family business. Our family business is a legacy, the foundation of which was laid by my late father, Mohsin Haider Darwish. It's our endeavour to take our family business to greater heights of success, and it's gratifying to see my son leading and redefining the family business. I am also proud of my family, as they are my pillars of strength. I am also gratified by the fact that I have been successful as a business leader by continuing our legacy and paving the way for MHD LLC towards continued excellence and success by diversifying the family business and expanding its brand portfolio across different sectors.

What does it take to be a successful woman these days? What are the three top things successful business people should personalise?
Success is very subjective. Some might perceive a high-profile career progression as a success, while others perceive a life filled with happiness and joy with family as successful. Irrespective of the essence, I think what it takes to be successful is diligence, focus, determination, continuous learning, determination to succeed, setting realistic and challenging goals. From the business perspective, I think women should set a vision and goals and plan on how to achieve their vision. Then, she should be willing to take risks and concentrate on the tasks that'll make a difference.

If the entire world listened to you for five minutes, what would you say or what would you want to talk about?
I would talk about gratitude. As humans, we often take things for granted. Yet gratitude is one of the vital elements of happiness. If we practice gratitude in our daily lives, we will be more optimistic, feel less stressed, and it also helps to see things from a different perspective.

Asila Al Musalhi

What has shaped you the most in your life? Is there any specific situation?
Seventeen years back, when I resigned from my previous organisation, I received an email forwarded by one of my ex-colleagues. They sent the email to all the staff by the top management, and it read, "We are welcoming someone who is going to replace Asila, but we know for sure that we can never replace her talent and commitment." I felt so touched, and this still motivates me to achieve in my career.

On the path to where you are now, what was the most determining step?
Before I take my turn at any point in my career, I make sure that I can advance in my career and that my role in that company is critical for its growth.

What do you respect most in other successful women?
I respect the fire and hunger for growth in the new generation of successful women. This motivates me to constantly update myself with new tools and knowledge that keep me up to date.

What would you recommend to a student just starting and dreaming of a successful career?
Think positive, stay focused and constantly pursue courses that will ensure you grow and you are able to climb up in your career.

If the entire world listened to you for five minutes, what would you say or what would you want to talk about?
My motto is to live and let live. In this current world of competition, we should be compassionate to others.

How would you describe your leadership style? What is your leadership motivation?
Teamwork.

If there is a lot of work and you are under stress, how do you compensate?
Stay organised.

Do you do anything to keep you fit physically or mentally, and how often?
Eat healthily and sleep well.

Head of Medical & Life / Oman Insurance Company

Which topics should humanity focus more on in the future?
Quality education for the women's population.

What does it take to be a successful woman these days? What are the three top things successful business people should personalise?
- Focus on your goal
- Creativity, optimism
- Self-motivation

What would you devote your time and energy to if you were to invest now, in your future best self?
Helping the community and supporting the less privileged.

What are your most important goals? Is there a difference for you between life goals and career goals?
Be more proactive. Yes, you can achieve a career goal one time, but you can achieve a life goal over and over again.

How would you describe yourself in three word, and what is your secret to success?
Creative, honest and ethical.
Time management and an organised personality make me successful.

Did the Omani culture you grew up in have an impact on your career path?
Our culture inspires us. I am proud to be Omani.

What is your favourite place in Oman, that you like to visit in order to relax and recharge your batteries?
Musandam and Masirah Island.

Asma Ali Al Zadjali

What was the best piece of advice that you were given regarding your career and that you will never forget?
Twelve years back, one of my mentors told me that it is essential to have a long-term career plan, create small steps to get there and be focused.

What has shaped you the most in your life? Is there any specific situation?
Having the right work-life balance. After I had my first child in 2009, this was one of my challenges for a long time. Balancing between the long hours required at the office, attending different academic programs, raising children and having a social life was one of the most challenging things in life. I was lucky to know the mentors' experience in this regard and got some coaching, which ultimately helped me manage this better.

Who would you identify as your role model? Whom do you look up to and why?
Jacinda Ardern, New Zealand Prime Minister, a young mother and leading a country, is one of my role models. Her presence, knowledge, and ability to take over such a senior role have motivated me in both problematic phases of my life. In our careers, we face many challenges, and looking around for women who have succeeded has always encouraged me.

What would you recommend to a student just starting and dreaming of a successful career?
I would recommend dreaming big, create a chart of that dream and start drawing the steps to get there. You may not have all answers or the clarity of how you will get there, but things will get clear with each step. Most important is to keep moving forward and, when required, take back a step to take two steps forward.

If the entire world listened to you for five minutes, what would you say or what would you want to talk about?
I want to talk about people's well-being and self-development. I would say that "Your career and your future are in your hands; plan it and work towards it. When you need help, get that help, but do not depend on others to make it for you. Also, check your progress and make necessary changes to your development as you move forward, and success will follow."

What essential qualifications do you think will be needed ten years from now?
With continuous changing times and the pandemic's start in 2020, the most critical future qualifications could be cognitive flexibility, digital literacy and computational thinking, artificial intelligence, emotional and social intelligence, innovation and technology related to the health sector.

How would you describe your leadership style? What is your leadership motivation?
I describe my leadership style as coaching. I help the team in unlocking their potential and work together with them in their career development plan. My motivation is to look back at many team members I was able to work with and develop.

General Manager, Head of Banking Operations Group / Oman Arab Bank SAOG

If there is a lot of work and you are under stress, how do you compensate?
I take a deep breath, read a good article, go out for a walk or have a quick chat with my mentor and get recharged.

What are the three things in life you are most proud of?
I am proud of my family, husband, and three daughters; proud of being able to mentor and coach people and at last proud to be optimistic, no matter what the situation is.

Do you do anything to keep you fit physically or mentally, and how often?
For being physically fit, I maintain a daily walking routine. For being mentally fit, I ensure to get help through coaching experience for my well-being.

If you had extra time of four hours a day, what would you do during that time?
I will add it all to 'Me Time' and read one book every day. As I am in the process of applying for DBA, these four hours may come in handy.

What are your most important goals? Is there a difference for you between life goals and career goals?
The most important goal is to continue developing myself to take over higher roles and help others achieve their goals. I don't see a difference in my personal and career goals as both move forward together.

How would you describe yourself in three words? Do you live with a daily routine, and what is your secret to success?
I take every day as it comes; yes, there is a daily routine. However, I am ok to change, revise as I move forward. The three words I would use to describe myself are strategic, optimistic, and being a coach. Being focused and always working closely with people has helped me to succeed.

What is your favourite place in Oman, that you like to visit in order to relax and recharge your batteries?
My 'Me Time' is my 5:30 am morning walk in Oman. This helps me recharge and get ready for the day.

Azza Al Ismaili

What was the best piece of advice that you were given regarding your career and that you will never forget?
Twenty years back, I submitted a piece of work. After reviewing the quality of it, my boss looked me in the eyes and said, "Before submitting any work, make sure it is accurate, and when you are sure, give it a second, final check." Since then, I have made it a habit to go through any task I'm completing at least twice.

What has shaped you the most in your life? Is there any specific situation?
To me, life is about learning from the different situations we face.
Back in 1995, during my first job. I joined a team comprising five male staff. When each one received the appraisal report, mine went, "... Azza is a great asset to the team; she has completed 2/3 of all the unit work." I was surprised and overwhelmed and realised that my ability to succeed is not limited; hard work and continuous effort pay off. So encourage yourself, even in challenging times, to stay positive, and this will make you stronger.

What would you recommend to a student just starting and dreaming of a successful career?
Take control of self emotions. You have a long journey up ahead of you; imagine a road that takes the letter 'W' shape, full of ups and downs. Therefore, the sooner you practice controlling your emotions while dealing with everyday challenges, the better. Through training your mind to be at peace at all times, you will become more calm and level-headed and, therefore, make better decisions towards achieving your goals.

How would you describe your leadership style? What is your leadership motivation?
Those who know me know that I am a people person. I have a solid ability to interact and listen to people's needs. I am an easy-going individual who positively affects others. I lead with my heart and am genuinely interested in supporting others and making them feel comfortable and secure. Situational leadership style would best describe it.

If there is a lot of work and you are under stress, how do you compensate?
I practice meditation every day, wake up one hour before sunrise, and start by saying my prayers. Then, I spend a few minutes at the end of my mediation counting my blessings, reminding myself of things I am genuinely grateful for. That helps me accept reality as it is. Furthermore, it encourages me to stay calm and not overreact to any situation. There are times

Founder & CEO / Azza Al Ismaili Group

when things seem to perturb. On those occasions, I do yoga and practice the art of detachment, wherein I let everything melt away and focus on the present moment and my breathing.

What are the three things in life you are most proud of?
- I have created over 650 jobs throughout my business.
- Being appointed as the Minister of Technology & Communications.
- Authoring the book "Oman-The Future Of Our History".

Do you do anything to keep you fit physically or mentally, and how often?
I work out about 5 to 6 times a week with my personal trainer, and also I exercise through various online courses. Exercising in a quiet space, surrounded by fresh air in my outdoor garden, helps boost my mind. Usually, I would spend the last ten minutes completing a mindful cooldown, mentally separating the parts of my day to manage any anxiety or stress. Finally, I would dedicate a few moments to be thankful for all that I have achieved, or learnt throughout the day, a simple exercise that very often serves as fuel to move me forward.

Is there a quote you favour that suits you? Or an important book you read that influenced you?
'Oman, The History of Our Future', a book that I was honoured to prepare and present to the Late Majesty, Sultan Qaboos Bin Said. The book consists of 5 main chapters; Introduction, Valuing our People, Valuing our Land, Valuing our Businesses, and Serving our People. I frequently refer to the book for my current and future projects.

What are your most important goals? Is there a difference for you between life goals and career goals?
I am passionate about securing a bright future for Oman. My primary focus is to bring together meaningful ideas and proposals that could address specific issues related to Omani people, businesses, and the environment. To keep me focused on achieving my goals, I developed an In-Country Value Framework that focuses on four main pillars:
- Products - to invest in products 'Made in Oman'.
- Services - to invest into 'Local Services'.
- Talent Management - to invest in local talents (with skill-sets needed to respond to future industrial challenges).
- Omanization - to invest in job creation for Omanis.

How would you describe yourself in three words? Do you live with a daily routine, and what is your secret to success?
Certain activities are part of my daily routine, such as waking up at a set time most days, exercising, reading, having dinner with my family, and going to bed at the same time. On the other hand, I am a person who is really into practising different things every day. Over the last 15 years, I founded about 11 companies in various businesses. I enjoy exploring new opportunities every day and continue pushing my limits and doing things outside my comfort zone.

(Dr.) Badria Al Shihhi

On the path to where you are now, what was the most determining step?
It was going for my higher studies right after my marriage. However, my husband encouraged me not to stop, and it was the right time before getting into making a family and other obligations that come with it.

Who would you identify as your role model? Whom do you look up to and why?
All strong and intelligent women are my role models. I love to see female high achievers. They work very hard to prove that, especially in societies that limit their role to family building.

What essential qualifications do you think will be needed ten years from now?
Social and emotional intelligence, paired with excellent communication skills, will be the best qualification or talent someone can have. Other skills, like technical knowledge, can be learnt on the go.

How would you describe your leadership style? What is your leadership motivation?
I am a person of transparency. I would straightforwardly confront my subordinates and colleagues, but I don't pick on minor items. I like the approach of thinking outside the box. I look more into effort and achievements to evaluate a person rather than time spent at the office. I appreciate intelligent and hardworking people and give them space to shine. As they shine, I shine too.

If there is a lot of work and you are under stress, how do you compensate?
I book a flight with my hubby for a week's vacation at a later time and start dreaming about it! That eases stress as I look forward to something I love. Alternatively, I go shopping or have lunch with a close friend.

What are the three things in life you are most proud of?
I was able to finish my masters and my PhD with two young kids.
Being able to do three jobs at once: an academic staff, administrative staff and a state council member. Additionally, write novels as time permits. Raise my kids to appreciate education and family ethics.

Do you do anything to keep you fit physically or mentally, and how often?
I insist on napping once a day for an hour. I believe it brings calmness and releases stress.

What are your most important goals? Is there a difference for you between life goals and career goals?
I always wanted to become a dedicated writer who travels the world and produces novels that show human beings' suffering and joy. But, unfortunately, my career so far contradicted that personal goal, which I keep delaying until the right time comes!

Deputy Chair of Oman State Council / Oman State Council

How would you describe yourself in three words? Do you live with a daily routine, and what is your secret to success?
No one can escape the routine. Any job, no matter how diverse it is, will eventually become a routine. I describe myself as a dedicated, sincere, and stubborn person. What makes me successful is that I never give up easily and I am transparent, and I think I am fair in general.

Did the Omani culture you grew up in have an impact on your career path?
I was lucky to have a family that was very understanding and accommodating. My father travelled and worked abroad from a young age, and hence he appreciated the value of education, choice, freedom and ambition.

What is your favourite place in Oman, that you like to visit in order to relax and recharge your batteries?
I like Jebel Akhdar. The mountains and the cooler weather fascinate me. I wrote two novels that take this place as the background space. It is because of the way it is isolated and structured. I enjoy the idea of complete isolation; it is a good chance to recharge and discover your inner self.

Badriya Al Siyabi

What was the best piece of advice that you were given regarding your career and that you will never forget?
A quote by Nelson Mandela, "I never lose, I either win or learn." I am very grateful to have come across this at an early age and career journey; I believe in it passionately, and it defined my thinking and motivation.

What has shaped you the most in your life? Is there any specific situation?
In 1994, I travelled to the USA for the first time to join a community centre in Golden, Colorado. During my stay, I learned that regardless of my colour or beliefs, I have to give back to the community I live in as to me social work and patriotism are unanimous!

On the path to where you are now, what was the most determining step?
Silencing the temptation of significant financial incentives in the banking sector and committing to my passion and purpose, so I took a job in a firm that shared my values. This decision has shaped who I am today. Following my passion will always outweigh financial motives.

Who would you identify as your role model? Whom do you look up to and why?
Oprah Winfrey's persona and presence appeal to me as I see so much in her that I can relate to. Modesty, honesty and empathy in her character that I admire. Specifically, transparency, as I realised and matured early to accept myself and embrace who I am. In addition, her dedication to empowering women, helping those in need and many selfless acts; has always touched me.

What do you respect most in other successful women?
The definition of 'success' can vary from one person to the other. I perceive success as a woman who can celebrate her femininity while adding value to societies and impact positive change on a global scale.

Founder of Sidab Women

What would you recommend to a student just starting and dreaming of a successful career?
Follow your heart always! Make the most out of your journey, take risks, move out of your comfort zone and always be thirsty for new experiences and challenges. If you are given the opportunity to work abroad, seize it! Most importantly, your personality is your main asset; let it reflect on your work and have a unique identity.

If the entire world listened to you for five minutes, what would you say or what would you want to talk about?
Sustainability should be at the core of our actions and decisions; we have a duty towards the earth and future generations. Change starts with oneself, and affecting others to do good should be a motive for greater change. Accepting that everyone is different and celebrating our differences is essential for creativity and innovation. Citizenships are not merely nationalities; they are distinctive identities that reflect unique identities.

What essential qualifications do you think will be needed ten years from now?
- Knowledge-based economy specialist.
- Communication skills in different, prominent languages.
- Career and life coaches.
- Business accelerators experts.

How would you describe your leadership style? What is your leadership motivation?
I perceive the team to be competent, so I expect tasks and responsibilities. Thus, they feel autonomous and, when in doubt, to learn from peers or by research. Thus, ensuring that a learning curve is reached at the end of a submission.

If there is a lot of work and you are under stress, how do you compensate?
I have realised that consistently working out and staying active helps me tame stress and anxiety. I am surrounding myself with a positive team and friends. Travelling frequently balances my work and personal time for better efficiency and concentration throughout the year.

What are the three things in life you are most proud of?
Proud to be Omani, proud to be a woman, proud of my values that reflect my personality without being pretentious.

Do you do anything to keep you fit physically or mentally, and how often?
I have a life coach, a career coach, and a personal trainer.

Baida Al Zadjali

What was the best piece of advice that you were given regarding your career and that you will never forget?
To always face challenges head-on. I have found that good communication is the key to resolving issues.

What has shaped you the most in your life? Is there any specific situation?
My childhood experiences living in metropolitan London during the Thatcher era. The combination of living in a multicultural environment, growing up seeing a female Prime Minister at the head of one of the most powerful governments in the world, and seeing my mother achieving her Masters in Dentistry.

On the path to where you are now, what was the most determining step?
It was deciding to study project management as my Master's after completing my Bachelor in Engineering. This completely opened a new pathway for me. It also made me realise that change can be positive. Another decisive moment was to start my own business. The life lessons from these two decisions have also changed my concept of wealth. Wealth is not necessarily about money. Instead, I found wealth in the freedom of choice, quality time with family, and the ability to pursue dreams. In a nutshell, be the best version of yourself.

Who would you identify as your role model? Whom do you look up to and why?
My mother. She became a single mom suddenly in a foreign country with three girls while completing her Master's degree. I admire her strength, resilience, and determination. I know in my heart that the strength and determination that got me through the most challenging times in life was what I had learnt from her.

What would you recommend to a student just starting and dreaming of a successful career?
To remain open to new possibilities, new pathways, and new horizons. To believe in yourself and make your dreams your reality. Always give your best shot at everything you do so you won't have any regrets.

If the entire world listened to you for five minutes, what would you say or what would you want to talk about?
It does not matter where you are from, who or what you are, male or female, tall or short, rich or poor, nothing matters, except your faith in yourself. Our biggest challenge is not our circumstances or inherent attributes; it's our mindset and ourselves.

What essential qualifications do you think will be needed ten years from now?
Conservation and the environment, artificial intelligence and robotics, critical thinking, and at least one artistic discipline to unlock our 'wild side' and imagination.

Managing Director Business / Meezah Engineering and
Project Management Consultants

If there is a lot of work and you are under stress, how do you compensate?
I always go back to nature; it is therapeutic and meditative. For example, when you go hiking, you think of the now, of the present, where your next step will be, and where your foot will land. Your mind is in a meditative state with only the present, and little other thought can cross your mind.

What are the three things in life you are most proud of?
I am proud to be a woman who shapes her destiny, being proud, compassionate, and dynamic. I rarely sit still! Walking 760 km across Oman Empty Quarter in 28 days on the first female-only walking team. Being elected as the first Arab Woman to the World Triathlon Women's Committee and starting Oman's first female-led Project Management Consultancy in Construction with my sister Noor.

Do you do anything to keep you fit physically or mentally, and how often?
I train for triathlons, so I swim, run, and cycle, and I also hike. I recently started training for an IRONMAN triathlon. Mentally, I write, meditate, and pray.

What does it take to be a successful woman these days? What are the three top things successful business people should personalise?
Integrity, resilience, and authenticity so that you never have to take a step backwards.

How would you describe yourself in three words, and what is it that makes you successful?
Strong, resilient, and giving. My sheer determination to achieve anything I set my mind to.

Did the Omani culture you grew up in have an impact on your career path?
Yes, and No. The culture as I finished university encouraged higher achieving students to pursue careers in medicine or engineering, so I chose engineering. After that, I moved to work in construction, which is uncommon in my culture.

What is your favourite place in Oman, that you like to visit in order to relax and recharge your batteries?
I love walking down to the pond near the dam, close to my house. The place has a diverse biological ecosystem with birds, foxes, and colourful dragonflies, all in a residential area in the middle of the city. It just feels like I am Alice stepping into Wonderland.

Balqees Al Hassani

What was the best piece of advice that you were given regarding your career and that you will never forget?
A former boss once told me, "It doesn't matter if you thought of it first; what matters is who wrote it down first." That ingrained in me the importance and value of my thoughts and cementing the idea that every one of us has a valuable narrative to contribute.

What do you respect most in other successful women?
All successful human beings, regardless of gender, are passionate, intelligent, ambitious, and focused on their goals. I've met people who are meant to be on a career path all over the place and stay-at-home parents who could run corporations with the ethos and commitment they manage their household and kids.

What would you recommend to a student just starting and dreaming of a successful career?
Unfortunately, there seems to be a mounting sense of pressure on young adults by their parents and educators to choose a knowledge stream that 'guarantees' gainful employment. Unfortunately, what is desirable in the job market today won't be tomorrow. Whatever high-paying jobs are relevant today may not even exist in five years. So, pursue an education for the love of knowledge or pursue a passion that you can pivot into an income.

What essential qualifications do you think will be needed ten years from now?
We live in a world where there seems to be a clear and focused direction towards more STEM-based qualifications, renewable energy, and alternative education methods. However, I hope the value of focusing on the creative arts, critical thinking, social & collaboration skills, interpersonal skills, etc., will not be diminished as these skills are what sets us apart from machines.

If there is a lot of work and you are under stress, how do you compensate?
Stop, and take half an hour to yourself. Have a coffee, take a brisk walk. I promise you the world will keep spinning, and your email inbox will continue to fill up! Never apologise for hitting the pause button when you feel overwhelmed; nothing compromises the quality of your work and performance, like exhaustion and poor mental health.

Which topics should humanity focus more on in the future?
Alternative Education Methods, as opposed to a focus on mainstream and standardised educational methods, environmental sustainability both on a corporate and governmental level, a clear focus on creating and encouraging entrepreneurship within the younger populations. More emphasis on interpersonal skills.

What does it take to be a successful woman these days? What are the three top things successful business people should personalise?
Focus, passion and ambition. These three are the foundation to building a successful corporate

and personal brand, regardless of your direction. I don't believe in that old conundrum of women not being able to 'have it all.' Instead, I think both men and women today realise the importance of having a healthy work/life balance. Each one helps to fuel the other.

What would you devote your time and energy to if you were to invest now, in your future best self?
In my personal opinion, there are only a handful of things that require you to invest your time and money: your health, your home, your education and yourself. To me, these are the best long-term investments any human being can make.

What are your most important goals? Is there a difference for you between life goals and career goals?
This will sound like an absolute cliché, but I find it to be true. The pursuit of happiness is the most important goal in your career, your personal life and within yourself. Granted, neither one of these three will ever be 'perfect' or free from a bit of mess here and there - but look at those little moments of contentment; when you're proud of a project you've submitted, or you've managed to spend an entire weekend with loved ones. Those are all little goals and 'wins' we should strive for.

How would you describe yourself in three words? Do you live with a daily routine, and what is your secret to success?
A little structure is essential to ensuring that you have all your bases covered throughout the day regarding your personal and corporate life. I believe in 30-minute intervals that will set the tone for the day. A 30-minute slot for myself in the morning, the same to prioritise team meetings and check in with staff and colleagues, and 30 minutes at the end of the day, so we have a good idea of what to expect for the next. A great deal of flexibility is required in every workplace, and having a little time carved out ensures everyone is plugged in and enthusiastic about participating.

Did the Omani culture you grew up in have an impact on your career path?
Growing up as Omani impacts how we all operate in the workplace despite our career choices. Striving for excellence, remaining humble, respectful, and understanding the importance of a rich and vast network are Omani social graces that translate well into the workplace.

Bothaina Al Zaabi

What was the best piece of advice that you were given regarding your career and that you will never forget?
Life is full of challenges, and to achieve my goals, I will always face obstacles. However, to avoid any demotion, I need to keep going and believe in doing. One should not stop; instead, learn from mistakes.

What has shaped you the most in your life? Is there any specific situation?
All my experiences throughout my life have shaped me into the person I am today. I am still on the journey, trying to figure out the most of my life. I consider all the difficulties I have gone through significant in shaping me in my career.

On the path to where you are now, what was the most determining step?
I have progressed a lot during these years. However, I believe that there is still a lot to be done, and I might not even reach half the path. The most decisive step was that I showed myself to the public and announced who was behind the OmanCareers initiative, as initially, I was doing it anonymously.

What essential qualifications do you think will be needed ten years from now?
Computing and Information Technology, Artificial Intelligence or Intelligent Systems. Physicians and Surgeons. Financial advisors and accountants. Engineering. Medicine and Healthcare. Environmentalism and climate change. However, I believe each country or economy has its needs based on the availability of resources.

How would you describe your leadership style? What is your leadership motivation?
I can say that I am inspiring others on how they should not give up their dreams. I try to give somebody the best advice they can hear and do what needs to be done.

CEO A'Riyadah Advanced Enterprises LLC

If there is a lot of work and you are under stress, how do you compensate?
Try to find a more straightforward solution or leave for five minutes and see everything from a new perspective. It is essential always to keep calm, find the best solution for the problems I face, and manage my time. As well as prioritise the tasks I am doing.

What are the three things in life you are most proud of?
My family: all the support, love and affection I get from my family is the best thing. OmanCareers initiative, a project that started from scratch and has helped many people in the community.

Completing my education being a housewife and at the same time achieving an outstanding degree. Do you do anything to keep you fit physically or mentally, and how often?
I exercise a few times a week as well as I meditate often. In addition, I drink enough water, play mind games, and spend time with people whose company I enjoy.

What does it take to be a successful woman these days? What are the three top things successful business people should personalise?
To become a successful woman, you will need a good idea, a good business plan and a solid set of core skills to help you do the work. In addition, you must be willing to learn and grow. Finally, be consistent and persistent and always ready to do your best. Know where to focus energy and time, network as much as possible, and make time for yourself.

What would you devote your time and energy to if you were to invest now, in your future best self?
I put my time into improving my skills and my business growth. If time is available, I should go for earning professional certificates or a Master's degree.

If you had extra time of four hours a day, what would you do during that time?
Read books, try to learn more, and try to engage more in worship. Also, I might try to learn new skills.

Did the Omani culture you grew up in have an impact on your career path?
Yes. My culture helped me understand what society requires and keep our costumes and traditions while modernising.

What is your favourite place in Oman, that you like to visit in order to relax and recharge your batteries?
Jabal Akhdar during Summer and Sharqiya during winter.

Diana Somar

What has shaped you the most in your life? Is there any specific situation?
Challenges, obstacles, and being independent. The major challenge was the financial support from the banks and government funding authorities.

Who would you identify as your role model? Whom do you look up to and why?
My role model was H. M Sultan Qaboos bin Said, as at the beginning of my career, I was given the honour to design and supply his palace with several items. Working close to a person like H. M made me be very precise and care about quality in every instance. Moreover, his vision towards Omani women made me proud and encouraged me to do more for my country.

What do you respect most in other successful women?
To balance work-life, and especially to become successful in both work and family. That is a notable achievement.

What would you recommend to a student just starting and dreaming of a successful career?
- Be strong and never give up
- Believe in yourself
- Choose the right path
- Study the market and be dynamic
- Pursue relationships with positive people
- Always consult experts.

If the entire world listened to you for five minutes, what would you say or what would you want to talk about?
I would talk about passion, patience and the impact of people in your life.

How would you describe your leadership style? What is your leadership motivation?
You can call it transformational leadership, and my leadership motivation is to inspire others with a vision that can create change.

What are the three things in life you are most proud of?
- Market reputation.
- Independency.
- Drawing smiles on people's faces, sending happiness.

Owner (CEO) / Diana Somar Perfumes

Which topics should humanity focus more on in the future?
Developing entrepreneurs and the importance of genuinely supporting them.

Is there a quote you favour that suits you? Or an important book you read that influenced you?
Implementing new ideas on people with old mentalities is a waste of time and effort.

If you had extra time of four hours a day, what would you do during that time?
More reading, self-development, and meditation.

Did the Omani culture you grew up in have an impact on your career path?
Yes, as I grew up in a culture that respects women, I was encouraged to choose my path freely. Moreover, part of the Omani culture was fashion and how every governance has its own unique style of dress, which influenced me initially.

So I became a fashion designer and participated in many international fashion shows. Then I moved to Jewellery and Perfumes, which are also a part of the Omani culture. So I was honoured to design jewellery for H. M at the beginning of my career and got an appreciation note.

What is your favourite place in Oman, that you like to visit in order to relax and recharge your batteries?
I love Al Jabal Al Akhdar, where nature meets heritage.

Fathiya Al Aisari

What was the best piece of advice that you were given regarding your career and that you will never forget?
"Growth happens outside your comfort zone."

What has shaped you the most in your life? Is there any specific situation?
I started working at a young age while studying at the same time. Therefore, I needed to organize myself very well and had much focus and motivation to manage it all.

Who would you identify as your role model? Whom do you look up to and why?
My role model is my father because he was one of the most hard-working and loving persons

I have ever met. He took care of me very well whenever I was in trouble, had confusion or was in tension. He then said to me, "Do what your heart says."

What do you respect most in other successful women?
Dedication, unity, ability to teach and learn from each other, responsibility, integrity, resilience and inspiring others.

What would you recommend to a student just starting and dreaming of a successful career?
Succeeding in college is rather like growing in life. It's much more about you than it is about college. So the most crucial place to start is to consider why you're here, what matters to you, and what you expect to get out of it. Even if you have already thought about these questions, it's good to reaffirm your commitment to your plan as we begin to consider what's involved in being a college student.

Finance Operations / Petroleum Development Oman

If the entire world listened to you for five minutes, what would you say or what would you want to talk about?
There is nothing impossible to achieve if you're genuinely into it and aim for it. So always plan ahead, write down your goals, have a positive attitude, and stay focused and motivated.

What essential qualifications do you think will be needed ten years from now?
Critical thinking and problem-solving, active learning, resilience, stress tolerance and flexibility.

How would you describe your leadership style? What is your leadership motivation?
I believe I have more of a visionary leadership style with a powerful ability to drive progress and usher in periods of change by inspiring employees and earning trust for new ideas. This helps to establish a solid organizational bond and strive to foster confidence among staff colleagues alike.

If there is a lot of work and you are under stress, how do you compensate?
I always try my best to alleviate heavy workloads by removing obstacles and clarifying priorities, improving team relationships by providing an outlet to give and receive feedback, promoting work-life balance, keeping employees motivated, allowing for breaks, and, most importantly, re-assess workload.

What are the three things in life you are most proud of?
Firstly, I am a proud working wife and mother of a beautiful daughter, proud of my 1st class honours degree double major in accounting and business, proud of being an international chartered accountant and proud of having such a supportive and loving family.

Do you do anything to keep you fit physically or mentally, and how often?
I get active, work out daily at least an hour at the gym or a simple jog, travel during my holidays, and always try to use the stairs instead of the lift.

Which topics should humanity focus more on in the future?
Teaching kids from a young age about handling finances, jobs, responsibilities, maintaining hygiene, and keeping our environment clean.

What does it take to be a successful woman these days? What are the three top things successful business people should personalise?
Know where to focus energy and time, learn how to hold yourself accountable, never fear asking for help. Don't ever be afraid to fail. Always be committed. You have to believe in yourself before anyone else will. Know your target audience. Never stop learning. Empower those around you. Develop thick skin but stay approachable and learn from mistakes.

(Dr.) Fatin Said Al Zadjali

What do you respect most in other successful women?

The humility they show and the genuine desire to serve communities. Successful women can form emotional connections in building partnerships. They have a common trait in focus, a sense of commitment and service for the interest of communities. Empathy is something that women possess naturally, and although we find ourselves accused of expressing emotions, it is this empathy that builds long-term connections for life.

What would you recommend to a student just starting and dreaming of a successful career?

I always coach students to unlock their potential and interests. Everyone has unique characteristics and can achieve what they desire, provided they are passionate about their goals. A successful career starts from within; I am amazed by some students who genuinely believe in their passion and pursue it relentlessly.

How would you describe your leadership style? What is your leadership motivation?

I feel that I am a participatory leader. I prefer working with groups and providing a sense of direction. I learnt it is necessary to consider all aspects before decision making. Questions are significant to understand, as well as listening. Allowing myself to make mistakes is also liberating if I place my intentions in the right connotation, and I learn from those mistakes. Most importantly, acceptance of oneself and desire to attempt, try and do rather than complain and blame. I am exploring my creative side and finding alternative ways to resolve matters efficiently and fairly.

Which topics should humanity focus more on in the future?

I am an avid sustainability supporter. I believe that we are still touching the surface on these deep-rooted issues. Sustainability and green practices should be a culture that is thought, celebrated, and embraced. It's time to act for the future of the next generations. An action-oriented approach could be weekly challenges, like living a zero-waste lifestyle or a vegan diet. Also, we need to reduce carbon emission, avoid dumping pollutants in the atmosphere and encourage farming. To claim that we are developed nations, we need to redefine the concept of development, to begin with.

What are your most important goals? Is there a difference for you between life goals and career goals?
There are several goals that I would like to pursue. Therefore, I divide my goals into subgoals. For each category, life goals contain my goals towards family, religion, and society. There are professional goals that include my career development and training.

Whereas I understand that some dreams are more challenging than others to achieve, I constantly pursue them to the best of my ability and see if they are meant to be or simply not. However, I allow myself to say that I have tried and haven't chickened up at the end of the day. Each goal I have is significant to me; therefore, I cannot prioritise one as they are different. However, family is the glass ball that I will constantly juggle to keep intact and value.

Did the Omani culture you grew up in have an impact on your career path?
I consider Omani culture as part of and parcel of the Omani businesswoman's identity. It nourishes the value propositions it entails, especially in terms of all for one and one for all. The responsibility towards the representation of Oman is also significant to understand how one can contribute best to bring the best traits, habits, and traditions of Oman in its business acumen.

A culture so enriched shapes the behaviour of its nation to the extent that the unified approach seems to be a dominant characteristic of the people of Oman. Omani culture stands for being tolerant, coexistent, and accepting. I am currently teaching, training, researching, consulting, and interacting with the youth of Oman to instil these core value propositions and pay them forward to the society and economy.

What is your favourite place in Oman, that you like to visit in order to relax and recharge your batteries?
Oman has a long coastline and beautiful, pristine beaches. The sound of crashing waves grounds me and provides a fresh perspective. Oman maintains its natural landscapes, just like a beautiful masterpiece of uninterrupted crystal-clear beaches. There are untouched water secrets within the Omani islands and an open invitation to explore what lies beneath those captivating shores.

Once you go down under, you discover marine life beyond your imagination. In the south Sharqiyah region, Oman maintains a turtle reserve home for an estimated 20,000 turtles nesting in the long 45k coastline.

(Dr.) Fatma Al Balushi

What was the best piece of advice that you were given regarding your career and that you will never forget?
Take whatever opportunities to learn, acquire knowledge, and strengthen your skills.

What do you respect most in other successful women?
I respect dedication and hard work. Women can truly inspire others and make a difference.

What would you recommend to a student just starting and dreaming of a successful career?
Accept whatever job opportunity you will get, and learn as much as you can.

If there is a lot of work and you are under stress, how do you compensate?
Prepare a to-do list every night, organise the tasks with the highest priority and then execute based on that.

What are the three things in life you are most proud of?
My family, my PhD degree, and my country.

Which topics should humanity focus more on in the future?
Oman 2040 vision is our future, and all efforts national wise should target it.

What does it take to be a successful woman these days? What are the three top things successful business people should personalise?
Reading. Mental and physical health. Good professional relationships. Give back to society.

Is there a quote you favour that suits you? Or an important book you read that influenced you?
"Education is the most powerful weapon which you can use to change the world."
Nelson Mandela

If you had extra time of four hours a day, what would you do during that time?
Learn a new language. Read more. Learn to play the piano.

Deputy Director-General of Administration and Financial Affairs / Oman Authority for Academic Accreditation and Quality Assurance of Education

How would you describe yourself in three words? Do you live with a daily routine, and what is your secret to success?
I am new at my current position, and it has not reached the daily routine stage for the time being. I am an ambitious, dedicated and fast learning person. I believe that being successful is not measured by myself; it should speak for itself. I dream BIG.

Did the Omani culture you grew up in have an impact on your career path?
Indeed, it was not easy for my mother and her friends to read and write back in those days, which inspired me to get my Ph.D. My mother was one of my biggest motivations for that step.

What is your favourite place in Oman, that you like to visit in order to relax and recharge your batteries?
My hometown, Shinas.

"Education is the most powerful weapon which you can use to change the world."

Nelson Mandela

Fatma Al Maimani

What was the best piece of advice that you were given regarding your career and that you will never forget?
The best advice for me was to work towards self-awareness in the early years; this helped me decide the best career path in line with my personality. Moreover, I followed Steve Jobs best advice to anyone, "Follow your passion."

What has shaped you the most in your life? Is there any specific situation?
I chose a challenging career path in the field of investment. In 2005, when I started my job, there were very few ladies working in this field. It's a very dynamic and return driven business environment. I faced many stressful periods, especially during economic turndowns. This helped me in stress management, not being afraid of such situations, and adapting to any changes. It also shaped me to develop myself constantly.

On the path to where you are now, what was the most determining step?
During my university days, I truly enjoyed most investments and portfolio management courses. I chose the investment path early on, and I never regretted choosing it as my career path. I also believe that the constant learning and building skills have impacted me both at work and personal levels.

Who would you identify as your role model? Whom do you look up to and why?
My role model is any woman worldwide who has never been afraid to follow her dreams, despite life's challenges. I took Oprah Winfrey as a clear role model to follow; she is such a great inspiration for many ladies and me worldwide.

In Oman, I would choose Sida Rawan Al Said. She is CEO and has been a chairman in a leading bank in Oman. She is a bright, cheerful, and confident lady.

What do you respect most in other successful women?
I respect the hard-working ladies who at the same time have a good balance between work and personal life. Furthermore, I appreciate the successful women who support other women, advise them and generally build up a working women's network and community.

What essential qualifications do you think will be needed ten years from now?
Every qualification related to technology would be essential for sure. The blockchain and cryptocurrencies are examples. I believe digitalization, in general, will shape our future in the following years.

Head of Investment Section / Royal Oman Police Pension Fund

If there is a lot of work and you are under stress, how do you compensate?
After 15 years of experience, I believe I am now more aware of managing work stress. Nevertheless, I tend to meditate and relax at home more. I also enjoy simple things such as walking, buying flowers, and cooking during stressful times. Simplicity in lifestyle helps me to overcome such stress.

What does it take to be a successful woman these days? What are the three top things successful business people should personalise?
Consistent work and self-awareness are the essential tools that can help women to be successful. Furthermore, patience, self-development, and networking are also important.

What would you devote your time and energy to if you were to invest now, in your future best self?
I would read more books and attend courses in different areas. I would also explore the universe, meet more interesting, successful people, and learn from their life experiences.

Did the Omani culture you grew up in have an impact on your career path?
Yes, a lot. Our government supports women in terms of issuing legislation that protects women's rights. Workwise, the government has assigned many leadership positions at the ministerial level to ambitious Omani ladies since the beginning. We live in a great business environment that believes in capabilities - regardless of gender. Another important aspect is my family, who encouraged me constantly and believed in my abilities.

What is your favourite place in Oman, that you like to visit in order to relax and recharge your batteries?
I like Musandam a lot; I went a few times, and I wish to go many more. It's an excellent destination to relax, enjoy great nature and do many sports activities. Musandam is the new government tourism target, and I wish people knew more about this beautiful place.

Fatma Said Al Sulaimani

What has shaped you the most in your life? Is there any specific situation?
My experience abroad played a crucial role in my personal and professional growth. It challenged me to go beyond my comfort zone and further reinforced my passion for HR and Brand Management. My key takeaways were never to build decisions based on face value and to strive to analyse and understand the complex underlying settings, risks, and potential impact.

Who would you identify as your role model? Whom do you look up to and why?
Many people with their unique characteristics inspired me. However, the key people are: In personal life: My parents ensured that we learn the real meaning of life and succeed in challenging situations and the importance of family and love. My husband raised my kids while I was away for my education and is equally ambitious in his field. In professional life: Her Excellency Maitha Al Mahrouqi is my role model. Her authenticity, journey, dedication and support for young leaders and local businesses inspire me.

What would you recommend to a student just starting and dreaming of a successful career?
There is no end to learning; use every opportunity in your life and always turn any negative thought or situation into a positive one by learning from it. Also, dream big and put all your dreams on a vision board that you can see each day. Look at it every morning and start your day positively, knowing that you will achieve your dreams.

Finally, don't allow anyone to stop you from achieving your goals and not compare yourself to others; your determination and success should come from the heart and your willingness to thrive against obstacles.

If the entire world listened to you for five minutes, what would you say or what would you want to talk about?
I would talk about the importance of empathy and emotional intelligence and how important it is to acquire these traits for young leaders. I would also talk about how it's essential to groom them by encouraging creative participation, embracing uncertainty, and leveraging diversity to strengthen the creative emergence of viable solutions.

Organization Development Manager / Oman Refreshment Company SAOG

How would you describe your leadership style? What is your leadership motivation?
I aspire and strive to exhibit a blend of transformational and diplomatic leadership styles;
I love working with different groups, creating a shared vision and fostering supportive relationships.

What are the three things in life you are most proud of?
I am proud of my life journey, as I truly believe that no journey is without its challenges.
I am proud of being selected as part of a prestigious higher education scholarship to study abroad.
That helped me learn educationally and from culture and life abroad.

I am proud of the moment I became a mother of my three children (Firas, Salma, and Sama). They
have taught me that life is positive by seeing it from a children's view - you always think of new ideas
and continue learning.

What does it take to be a successful woman these days? What are the three top things successful
business people should personalise?
It is essential to work on self-improvement continually, never stop learning or reading, and be up to
date with the world news. Also, a successful woman always takes the initiative. The words "can't do"
should be out of her dictionary. She always surrounds herself with positive people and like-minded
friends who think of moving successfully towards the future.

In my opinion, the three top things successful businesspeople should personalise are:
- Be fearless of starting a new business. Always think outside the box and don't be a
  cookie-cutter and copy the existing trades around.
- Be a leader and focus on emotional intelligence.
- Be positive and know your surroundings.

Is there a quote you favour that suits you? Or an important book you read that influenced you?
There is no such thing as impossible; when there is a will, there is a way.

How would you describe yourself in three words, and what is your secret to success?
My eagerness to learn and the drive to complete my projects perfectly on time make me successful.
I am energetic, self-motivated, and ambitious.

Did the Omani culture you grew up in have an impact on your career path?
The culture I grew up in was very inclusive; our parents treated all my siblings' equally. Education
was on top of the agenda, and the bar for performance was set very high. We were brought up on
principles of defending our rights, discipline, time management, respecting others and intervening if
something goes wrong.

Fatma Sulaiman Al Azri

What was the best piece of advice that you were given regarding your career and that you will never forget?
"Keep learning and keep reading."

On the path to where you are now, what was the most determining step?
My education was the most decisive step. That includes my MBA qualification and my B. Sc. Industrial Engineering.

What do you respect most in other successful women?

- She has balance in her life.
- She has integrity.
- She is strong-minded.
- She can overcome obstacles.
- She has a positive attitude.

What would you recommend to a student just starting and dreaming of a successful career?
- Have goals.
- Attitude.
- Stay focused and motivated.
- Plan ahead.
- Prioritise.
- Choose a role model.

What essential qualifications do you think will be needed ten years from now?
In my opinion, it will be the following skills: Analytical thinking and innovation, active learning and learning strategies, and complex problem-solving.

If there is a lot of work and you are stressed - how do you compensate?

- Start my day off right.
- Be clear on requirements.
- Stay away from conflicts.
- Stay organised.
- Be comfortable.
- Listen to music.
- Good coffee.
- Going for a walk.

**Director of External Office Affairs / Ministry of Commerce,
Industry & Investment Promotion**

Do you do anything to keep you fit physically or mentally, and how often?
Yes, I do. I go to the gym at least four times a week. I also love to walk on the beach and connect with nature.

What does it take to be a successful woman these days? What are the three top things successful business people should personalise?
- Self-belief.
- Ambition.
- Confidence.
- Passion.
- Humility and a willingness to learn.
- Hard work.
- Bravery.
- Persistence.
- Assertiveness.

What would you devote your time and energy to if you were to invest now, in your future best self?
Use more time to improve my skills and capabilities.

How would you describe yourself in three words? Do you live with a daily routine, and what is your secret to success?
I would describe myself being hardworking, energetic and intelligent. No, I don't.
I would name the following words to describe what makes me successful:

Self-beliefambition, confidence, passion, humility, willingness to learn, hard work, bravery, persistence and assertiveness.

Did the Omani culture you grew up in have an impact on your career path?
Yes, it did.

What is your favourite place in Oman, that you like to visit in order to relax and recharge your batteries?
I like the beach and also the mountains.

Fatma Sultan Bahwan Al Mukhaini

What was the best piece of advice that you were given regarding your career and that you will never forget?
My mentor said to me, "Don't forget to enjoy the ride rather than just living it." These words always remind me of why I do what I do and bring back my passion.

What has shaped you the most in your life? Is there any specific situation?
Trusting myself. At the start of my career, I wasn't sure of my talent in management and operations. However, after a while, I started seeing how my work impacted our efficiency as our operations expanded with new members joining the space. I had to come up with better systems and better ways to manage our resources, and seeing things go into motion made me realise how much of an impact I can make.

Who would you identify as your role model? Whom do you look up to and why?
I look up to different people in the way they handle specific situations.
When dealing with demanding situations with grace, I would name my mentor Mr Khalid Al Huraibi; he taught me that challenging situations make us stronger and facing them head-on is the only way to do it. I also look up to my best friend "Amel" in her constant desire to be a better version of herself.

What do you respect most in other successful women?
Successful women always give back to their communities even before they are seen as 'successful'. They have a close relationship with the communities they work in. You'll see them in events, charity activities, talks, etc. - to give back, whether it's by sharing knowledge, providing opportunities or other means.

What would you recommend to a student just starting and dreaming of a successful career?
Start early and imagine the type of career you want to build! Then arm yourself with the right kind of skills and personality traits. No matter how young you are, build your confidence in

what you want to be, be passionate about it and don't be afraid to speak of it from day one, and it will speak for you as you develop.

How would you describe your leadership style? What is your leadership motivation?
I'm more of the type that pushes her team to explore new limits; I'd push them to love what they do and do it with a passion, so they come to work excited about getting things moving. Also, the more space we give our team to explore their strengths and weaknesses, the better they become and their productivity.

What are the three things in life you are most proud of?
Myself! My co-founders, Mohammed & Omar, we've spent our youth building something we didn't know would work. Al Rud'ha brand, how we created a new working culture in Oman.

Do you do anything to keep you fit physically or mentally, and how often?
Yes! I'm a very optimistic person by nature. So, when I'm stressed, I don't hide it; I express it with words, music and the occasional walks in my neighbourhood and allow myself to feel drained and exhausted until it's entirely out of my system. Then my energy goes back up naturally.

What does it take to be a successful woman these days? What are the three top things successful business people should personalise?
I think a positive attitude is a significant factor towards being successful for both women and men. Perseverance is also a key trait of successful people, and I feel it's not as spoken about as it should be. Success is not made in a day or month - it is the ability to endure and persevere. To have a community that believes in what you do would be supporting.

Is there a quote you favour that suits you? Or an important book you read that influenced you?
"I believe that hard work can surpass the work of a born genius", it's a quote from the Anime Naruto that resonated with me, and it pushed me to always work hard for what I want even if there was some-one out there that could do the same effortlessly.

Did the Omani culture you grew up in have an impact on your career path?
I grew up in an environment where ideas, concepts and mistakes are part of our daily conversations with my parents and siblings. I was always pushed to join more activities and make new friends, and that acted as an open field to explore & understand myself more, build my own relationships and choose the community I wanted to be part of. I think this has essentially made it easy for me to become the person I am today.

Ghaya Al Barwani

What was the best piece of advice that you were given regarding your career and that you will never forget?
When I was in school, the first advice was from my father. "You cannot always do what you love, but you can always love what you do; so, choose to love what you do." The second piece of advice came from Dr Abhijit Das (specialised in Behavioural Sciences Training, Black Belt in Mixed Martial Arts, with two Masters Degrees and an M. Phil. in Music). When I asked him how he managed all that, he told me, "I give 100%, I do not treat anything like a hobby." That taught me to dedicate 100% to everything I do.

What has shaped you the most in your life? Is there any specific situation?
My great-grandmother's sister, Dr Fatma Salim Al Maamari, was the second Arab woman to receive a PhD, and she was the woman who raised my father. I remember when I was going to university, my father told me, "Mama Fatma was the first woman in our family to get a PhD, you are going for your bachelor's degree; you aren't the first, and you won't be the last; just be the best you that you can be." It took away any pressure I may have felt and allowed me to focus on just being me, the best me I can be.

What would you recommend to a student just starting and dreaming of a successful career?
Dream big! Dream colossal! Then set deadlines for those dreams to turn them into great goals! Every time you achieve one dream, target the next one and pay it forward. In the same way, you receive support on your journey. Help others on theirs.

What essential qualifications do you think will be needed ten years from now?
With increased job automation and machine learning and the rise of the gig economy, there seems to be a growing concern that humans may become redundant. However, I read a report by Deloitte that showed that this fear is not entirely justified. The report highlighted that human skills, such as empathy, creativity, and collaboration, will still be needed in the future.

Do you do anything to keep you fit physically or mentally, and how often?
Every day I make sure I take at least five minutes to move my body, to keep me physically fit, five minutes to meditate, to keep me spiritually grounded, five minutes to connect with loved ones, to keep me emotionally stable and five minutes to read to help me stay mentally sharp.

What does it take to be a successful woman these days? What are the three top things successful business people should personalise?
Acknowledge your strengths and areas for improvement. My questions to every leader, male or female, are as follows:
- What is your focus?
- What do you want to accomplish and why?
- What are your strengths?
- What are you doing right to help you achieve your goal (s)?

Corporate and Business Leadership Coach and Trainer

Dream big! Take your focus and magnify it ten times, 100 times, 1000 times! Draw up your action plan using your creativity, innate strengths, and talents. Now focus on the first step! In short, dream big and keep your focus, then take one step a day to help get you there, and you finally will!

What are your most important goals? Is there a difference for you between life goals and career goals?
My most important goal is to leave this world the same as I found it, if not better! As a coach, I support Business Leaders who feel like they live a life that keeps them trapped. A primary reason for this feeling is that they have centred their focus on professional and financial goals. Instead, they should balance things out to incorporate ALL of who they are: family members, friends, spouses, colleagues, community members and, most importantly, individuals. In my opinion, career goals are excellent motivators when combined with all areas of life, relationships, spiritual & community service and individual wellbeing.

How would you describe yourself in three words? Do you live with a daily routine, and what is it that makes you successful?
I live my life with focus; I give 100% to whatever I am doing as I am doing it. I describe myself as a Gypsy-Bedouin Islander in a Suit! Accepting all of who I am and overcoming the need to keep the Gypsy, the Bedouin, the Islander, and the Suit separate helped me succeed.

Did the Omani culture you grew up in have an impact on your career path?
Oman is who I am. My family hails from Sharqiyah, with strong women and stronger men! One of my female ancestors used to purchase artillery from East Africa, travel to Ibra and on her way there sell the ammunition to different tribes and people before arriving in Sharqiyah and donating the rest to her tribe. Oman and Omani women are strong, resilient, resourceful, adaptable, and intelligent. I hail from a sound foundation that is Oman!

What is your favourite place in Oman, that you like to visit in order to relax and recharge your batteries?
I love the coasts of Oman, the Wahiba desert and the serene caves and mountains. I adore the colours of the soil of Oman, from the white sandy beaches of Salalah to the orange sands of Wahiba and the grey mountains that protect its shores. I love the diverse natural ocean dwellers and the rich desert culture.

Hanaa Al Hinai

What was the best piece of advice that you were given regarding your career and that you will never forget?
At the start of my career, I was a financial advisor in Melbourne, Australia. I was taught very early that to become successful in gaining my customer's trust in my advice, was to put myself in their shoes. It allowed me to see things from their perspective. Build empathy and see what they may have gone through and how to better assist them in moving on with their lives with a better financial plan at hand. I started to apply this advice to every situation and person. I always try to put myself in their shoes.

What has shaped you the most in your life? Is there any specific situation?
From the early age of 17, I lived abroad for ten years, completing my Bachelor and Master and also gained seven years of working experience, mainly in the financial advisory industry. With this experience, I gained independence and confidence, which shaped my life path. It made taking on new challenges a lot easier. My perception of the world also changed as I experienced much diversity. This enabled me to develop a solid international network, which helped me work for some multinational companies. Lastly, I started to believe that there is no limit to what you can achieve in your life, which enabled me to get to where I am today in my career and personal life.

What do you respect most in other successful women?
Their acceptance that "You Can't Do it All Every day!" I'm a firm believer that as a woman, you "Can have it all", but you can't "Do it All Every day". Some days we have to dedicate more hours to work, some days we have to dedicate more hours with the family, some days we have to save some time for ourselves to recharge, and some days we need to dedicate time to our friends. But we can NOT dedicate every day to all the above. It just doesn't work that way in the long run.

What would you recommend to a student just starting and dreaming of a successful career?
The world is your oyster; you and you alone can take what life throws at you and turn it into a positive experience. Own everything that you do, own your decisions, own your choices and

Deputy Chief Executive Officer UAE & Bahrain / RSA Middle East

own the outcomes. Make the most of every opportunity and work hard to become the best at what YOU do. Whatever career path you decide to pursue or whichever business venture you wish to start, try to be the best at just that. Don't try to be everything and do everything all at one go. Instead, focus on what makes you (or your business) different, unique, desirable, and successful.

What essential qualifications do you think will be needed ten years from now?
The World Economic Forum predicts that we will need to reskill more than 1 billion people by 2030, as the Fourth Industrial Revolution transforms jobs: existing jobs and future jobs not created yet. Some of the skill sets required that will be critical attributes for our future growth are data skills, artificial intelligence, Blockchain, emotional intelligence and creativity, to name a few. In addition, healthcare qualifications are also an essential attribute to our future growth due to the global ageing population.

If there is a lot of work and you are under stress, how do you compensate?
I learned very early on the necessity to delegate the right task to steam members, who were the most effective in getting the job done. This relieved a lot of stress for everyone. What was most effective for my team was to lead them by removing obstacles in their way, getting approvals, motivating them, and rewarding them.

What are the three things in life you are most proud of?
I am proud of my family and friends and how we have all grown and evolved throughout the years. I am proud of what I have achieved throughout my career and the people's lives that I have shaped and inspired. Finally, I am proud of having learnt how to see things from another person's perspective, which has helped me help others whether in my professional career, coaching or just being a friend.

Do you do anything to keep you fit physically or mentally, and how often?
I exercise 2-3 times a week and try to walk as much as I can. This helps to keep me physically fit. To mentally keep fit, I like to go for a massage once in a while or have some ME time, even if it's just for 10 minutes. So, I can gather my thoughts and take a mental break from the world.

Did the Omani culture you grew up in have an impact on your career path?
Quoting the words of his late Majesty, Sultan Qaboos bin Said, "No nation can realize its goals unless its people work together to build its future and develop its potential.

We are confident that all of you-both men and women-will play your part in developing and building up this Omani enterprise, reinforcing its roots and raising its structure." As an Omani woman, these words have always inspired me to think big and not limit myself to what I can achieve for myself and my country's success.

Hanaa Mohammed Al Kharusi

What was the best piece of advice that you were given regarding your career and that you will never forget?
"Challenge yourself to come out of your comfort zone!" That advice made me take a career turn very early on, which I am very grateful for (I was a Microbiology Major who pursued a career in banking). As human beings, we tend to get comfortable and complacent. We tend to underestimate our capabilities and question our self-confidence, so a reflection and nudge are required to extract the best out of a person's life from time to time.

What has shaped you the most in your life? Is there any specific situation?
Trusting parents who have guided me and allowed me to study abroad and become independent. Growing up, I was a very shy and sensitive girl and had the underlying capabilities only revealed when needed. Being made to take responsibility was the proper challenge that I am thankful for, as it built on my self-confidence, resilience, and flexibility.

What do you respect most in other successful women?
The ability to inspire/guide and motivate other women to succeed, as women tend to be very competitive. That earns the respect of others and demonstrates the humility of their achievement and utilising their success to have a positive impact.

What would you recommend to a student just starting and dreaming of a successful career?
I would recommend taking every opportunity that you stumble across and using it as a learning experience. Realise that every exposure, no matter how simple or mundane, is a learning opportunity to develop a skill. Embrace the challenges you face in today's world and continue with a positive approach. Identify a mentor who can guide you with perseverance, hard work, and a positive attitude; a successful career is ahead of you.

If the entire world listened to you for five minutes, what would you say or what would you want to talk about?
I would talk about how countries, businesses and leaders need to consider the human element in their pursuance of power and wealth. There is enough to go around for everyone in this world, and if we can address inequality, pursuing those elements would be more reasonable.

If there is a lot of work and you are under stress, how do you compensate?
Take a time out and step back to reflect on what I am doing; take the time to prioritise what I do. Often, it is not the load of work that causes stress but the approach taken. I always talk to someone; sometimes, the obvious and simple might be overlooked because of anxiety. De-stress is sometimes required, and everyone has their unique way of dealing. A time out at the beach or spa and extra fun times with the children are sure to de-stress.

General Manager & Head of Corporate Banking / Ahlibank SAOG

Do you do anything to keep you fit physically or mentally, and how often?
Yes, I exercise a few times a week, alternating between indoors and outdoors. While physical and mental fitness is often asked about separately, physical fitness is a key enabler to mental fitness. I achieve my mental fitness through prayer and talking to my sisters, appreciating achievements and accomplishments, understanding that everything considered "gone wrong" has happened for a reason and has a learning curve behind it. Maintaining positive relations with family, friends and colleagues and re-acknowledging your purpose in life promotes positivity and helps in the journey towards optimum mental health.

What are your most important goals? Is there a difference for you between life goals and career goals?
Making a difference in anything I do with a positive impact. Whether it's closing a successful project financing, landing a competitive deal, achieving profitability as well as the ROE shareholders are looking for, my career goal is to contribute positively to the economy and make a leadership impact that inspires others. Life goals are similarly helping the people around me, ensuring my children have a positive role model that guides them to impact society and the world we live in. The end goal is to make my existence worthwhile in my organisation, community, country, region, and world.

How would you describe yourself in three words? Do you live with a daily routine, and what is your secret to success?
Yes, absolutely. My life is routine-based, and other than the occasional spontaneous outing; I like it that way. My success comes from extracting the positivity around me and trying to re-frame every challenge I come across. Maintaining positive relationships and being composed in situations where anxiety is typically caused has been the key to success.

What is your favourite place in Oman, that you like to visit in order to relax and recharge your batteries?
Ritz Carlton spa and beach at Bustan palace, a distinct wellness experience, is required from time to time.

Haritha Salim Al Busaidi

On the path to where you are now, what was the most decisive step?
Always be looking to the next step forward in my career because I started to plan what's next from day one.

What do you respect most in other successful women?
A woman may always be characterised by a multiplicity of aspirations, capabilities and energies, as a woman can do more than one job simultaneously. A successful woman can balance professional, work and family life and not neglect any aspect of them. After her long day at work, she sees her, after returning home, wearing another hat to start a different job than the work she used to do in the morning. In addition, women provide support and assistance to those around them and encourage them to reach their goals, guided by their successes and achievements. The woman has a comprehensive and loving heart; she presents with love and, without feeling jealous, that someone else can reach what she has achieved.

What would you recommend a student just starting and dreaming of a successful career?
Continuously pursue your dreams, follow your own path in life, and you will find something you excel in your life. The world is enough for everyone. Therefore we complete each other. So let us make the earth a better place to live.

What essential qualifications do you think will be needed ten years from now?
Digital technologies skills, Digital literacy and computational thinking, Data skills, Creativity, Artificial intelligence, Emotional Intelligence, Creative and innovative mindset, Fourth Industrial Revolution, Automation and machine learning, Self-management skills, Critical thinking and problem-solving skills, Emotional and social intelligence, Judgement and decision-making, Cognitive flexibility, Block chain.

If there is a lot of work and you are stressed - how do you compensate?
Sometimes, it happens to me when I am in the office, and many files are on my table, and I don't know where to start. So, the first step is to organise the files, papers on my desk, rearrange the place in general. Then I can light a candle, make myself a cup of green tea, and start arranging the work from least important to very important. Of course, I start with the easy and small work that can be accomplished quickly to reduce the files on the table, and I do not mean here underestimating the essential or urgent files that may require me some focus a longer time. Therefore, after I finish my cup of green tea, I can start with the critical and high priority files.

Do you do anything to keep you fit - physically or mentally?
I will not say, as many others say, that I exercise daily or I'm committed to some activities, I hope to do that and try, but I do not persevere. I practice yoga in addition to walking sometimes. Also, I like reading some books and novels if the opportunity arises. On the other hand, I practice some other hobbies such as cooking and preparing desserts and cakes for occasions and organising parties for the family members.

**Director, Organizations & International Relations Department /
Oman Chamber of Commerce & Industry**

Which topics should humanity focus more on in the future?
During his first speech in February 2020, Sultan Haitham bin Tariq highlighted the importance of Omani youth by saying: "Young people are the wealth of our nation, they are our present and our future, and we are eager and sincere to listen to them." Therefore, it is crucial to listen to their issues and point of view on how they see their country's future. They are the nation's builders, and it is imperative to listen to them and engage in an appropriate scientific dialogue. Also, addressing the high unemployment rate by empowering Omani youth is critical at this stage.

What does it take to be a successful
woman these days? What are the three top things successful business people should personalise?
Be organised and tidy up, be punctual, be kind and supportive, and be sociable and willing to listen. Set measurable goals that you can check off as you achieve them. You can break your big goals into small ones once that you can measure them.

Don't focus on problems, but focus on solutions. Accept that you can't control and do everything by yourself (delegate if possible).

Are you living within a daily routine? How would you describe yourself in three words? What is your secret to success?
I don't live in a daily routine; I have much work to do as my career has many tasks and challenges, it is renewable, varied and I enjoy it. As well as for my family life, we are trying to renew our daily life and do our best to introduce new activities to create positive energy. I'm an organised person, punctual, kind and supportive, and sociable and willing to listen.

I believe in what Bill Gates said: "I am not in competition with anyone but myself. My goal is to improve myself continuously." And we have to take in mind what John Wooden said: "Success is peace of mind which is a direct result of self-satisfaction in knowing you made an effort to become the best that you are capable of becoming."

So, it's essential to work hard and do your best, but it's important also to remember that life itself is not a competition. Compete can yield business success, but challenging yourself in healthy ways while feeling empowered can deliver joy and happiness.

Haura Al Wahaibi

What was the best piece of advice that you were given regarding your career and that you will never forget?
"Growth happens outside your comfort zone." This advice has motivated me through the most challenging times of my life at professional and personal levels.

What would you recommend to a student just starting and dreaming of a successful career?
I would highly encourage students to take charge of their own lives, whether academic or social journeys. By taking ownership of their path, they exercise leadership roles to prepare them for life outside academia. Whilst being a student at the university, they can participate in students' campaigns and societies to develop their leadership skills.

If the entire world listened to you for five minutes, what would you say or what would you want to talk about?
I would love people worldwide to accept differences and tap into their similarities as human beings, hence building a greater level of tolerance towards humanity.

Director of Investment Promotion / Ministry of Commerce, Industry & Investment Promotion

How would you describe your leadership style? What is your leadership motivation?
I am motivationally driven by Stephen R. Covey's profound statement, asserting that "[t]rust is the confidence born of the character and competence of a person or an organization". Thereby, I first seek to identify the talents of my teamwork, tap into these skills, and delegate their tasks accordingly. Then, by giving my team the trust they deserve, they can soar!

Do you do anything to keep you fit physically or mentally, and how often?
I tend to exercise regularly to maintain my physical and mental health simultaneously. I do also practise meditation. At other times, I embrace solitude to regain my balance across the board.

Which topics should humanity focus more on in the future?
Topics that should have more focus in the future are the following:
Investment, entrepreneurship, and technology.

What would you devote your time and energy to if you were to invest now, in your future best self?
I would definitely invest in my higher education and hone my academic and practical skills.

If you had extra time of four hours a day, what would you do during that time?
I would spend my time reading and thus keeping abreast with the latest theoretical and technological changes in business, international communication, investment, and leadership.

How would you describe yourself in three words and what is your secret to success?
It is resilient; I am a lifelong learner, as well as a highly dynamic individual.

Did the Omani culture you grew up in have an impact on your career path?
As you know, Oman has varying cultural matrices, synergizing splendidly. Such bent cultures have profoundly impacted my personality, thus developing cross-cultural perspectives and communications, which greatly help me blend in effortlessly.

What is your favourite place in Oman, that you like to visit in order to relax and recharge your batteries?
I love hiking in the mountains, as these places are enveloped in serenity.

Huda Hamed

What was the best piece of advice that you were given regarding your career and that you will never forget?
In the world of writing, I will never reach the top, so I will enjoy the road and the journey.

What has shaped you the most in your life? Is there any specific situation?
I was a dreamy girl in a small village, writing the words "I will be a writer" in my diary. But that was the reason I was being bullied. After I read the novel "Little Women", where one of the sisters, her name was "Jo", was writing despite the war, it was precisely what gave me hope, and I followed my dream.

On the path to where you are now, what was the most determining step?
When I came out of my small village after high school and went to the Republic of Syria for university studies, I discovered that the world, stories and ideas are more than I thought. I watched movies, went into public libraries, and attended the theatre for the first time in my life.

Who would you identify as your role model? Whom do you look up to and why?
There is no definite character; it changes from time to time. But I like writers who are good at moving our emotions with their words. They make us look at our lives profoundly and contemplate.

What do you respect most in other successful women?
I respect women who do not succumb to difficult circumstances. I respect women who break chains more than women who play the victim.

What would you recommend to a student just starting and dreaming of a successful career?
I would say you might fall many times, cry, and lose confidence in some people, but the truth you shouldn't miss is: always follow your dream.

How would you describe your leadership style? What is your leadership motivation?
I don't know if I can claim to be an influential person. But I can say that writing is one of the soft forces that influence the way of thinking in life. When I write articles in newspapers and magazines on issues related to women, for example, this raises many dormant questions and thus a state of enriching controversy. This is what motivates me to keep moving ideas.

If there is a lot of work and you are under stress, how do you compensate?
I escape to a café with a selected book. Or I go to the cinema, and sometimes I leave my children at their grandmother's and travel with my husband, who has similar interests. After that, I would be ready to jump back into my stressful daily routine.

Writer & Journalist

What are the three things in life you are most proud of?
Proud first that I studied at a time when it was difficult for girls. I am proud to have married a man who understands me and appreciates my work as a writer. Thirdly, I am proud of my children and my attempts to enjoy life.

Do you do anything to keep you fit physically or mentally, and how often?
Sports, Zumba, music, escape from the city to the childhood village.

What does it take to be a successful woman these days?
What are the three top things successful business people should personalise?
Women should be less concerned about how society views them. However, a successful woman should find support from deep inside, not wait for it from others.

Is there a quote you favour that suits you? Or an important book you read that influenced you?
The French writer Annie Ernault says, "The function of writing is not to obliterate or heal a wound but to give it meaning and value and make it unforgettable."

What are your most important goals? Is there a difference for you between life goals and career goals?
My goals are not clearly defined as my priority is to enjoy life and career experience away from hectic objectives' pursuing. Although, we can't deny that this last negative idea is the exact one that pushes us to chase our dreams.

Did the Omani culture you grew up in have an impact on your career path?
Omani culture is very involved in my novels and stories. Especially those old stories related to the world of magic and exoticism. Oman has a fertile imagination that has not yet been reproduced well, artistically and in writing.

What is your favourite place in Oman, that you like to visit in order to relax and recharge your batteries?
I love the sea and the high mountains like Jabal Shams.

Ibtisam Alkhaifi

What was the best piece of advice that you were given regarding your career and that you will never forget?
Go after experience and not job titles.

What has shaped you the most in your life? Is there any specific situation?
Dedication and commitment to the plans I make. Planning your career and life is essential. But what is more important is staying committed to your goals and follow them through until they become results and dreams come true. The second thing is getting outside my comfort zone, getting into new situations, and doing things that I have not done before to speed up my learning curve and learn new things every time.

On the path to where you are now, what was the most determining step?
The most decisive step was when I decided to leave the full-time job many dreamed of and started my own business. It was a calling deep from my inner soul that I couldn't ignore. So, I did, and I am happy that I did. Taking risks is crucial to turn around and succeed rather than following a standard, secure path that might not give you enough growth.

Who would you identify as your role model? Whom do you look up to and why?
There are many role models I have in my life. One of them is my late grandmother. She did not receive a formal education, but she was very educated, knowledgeable and sharp. She lived most of her life in rural areas. I remember telling her once in my 1st career in an oil company that I am the only woman in my team working with many men, which makes me feel uncomfortable. But, she said, "The daughter of true men doesn't fear other men". So, from that time, I took on all challenging roles in my career. The second role model that I always look up to is Ms Haifai Al Khaifi. I worked once as part of her leadership team, and I've been very inspired by her ever since. She is a powerful, strategic, and ambitious woman.

What would you recommend to a student just starting and dreaming of a successful career?
Take as much experience as you can. Explore many career opportunities. Be involved in different roles or take on new projects and assignments until you find your strength and focus on it after that. Getting the right foundations to become successful in the future is vital.

What are the three things in life you are most proud of?
I am proud of who I am; I have high values and ethics and am an initiator. I have inspired many women around me. I am also proud of maintaining my hobbies and physical health despite my commitment to work. As a woman, my focus is also on my family and kids.

In early 2020 I ran 20 KM in the Muscat marathon in only 3 hours. Later, I realised I was pregnant (1.5 months) with my second son. As a working mum and being fit, I think this shows

Founder & CEO / Simat Human Development LLC

how much we women hold power within, mentally and physically. Being rewarded "Middle East Women Leader 2020" from the World Leadership Women Congress made me very proud.

Do you do anything to keep you fit physically or mentally, and how often?
I exercise 3 times a week, from a simple walk to an intense strength exercise. In addition, I do yoga now and then because it helps remove body pain caused by work stress.

What does it take to be a successful woman these days? What are the three top things successful business people should personalise?
It takes confidence and belief in oneself. Being different and holding unique attributes is a differentiating factor. The workplace, politics, and business all need women's unique talents and skills. If you also see that there are countries with women very much involved in the political, educational, and economic sectors and were able to advance on a faster pace. Women should know their uniqueness and use it to improve the world. There is no need to compete with men; we need to support them to make this world better for everyone.

How would you describe yourself in three words? Do you live with a daily routine, and what is your secret to success?
Getting the most out of early morning is one of the contributors to my achievement. We have a saying that wealth and success are distributed in the morning and if you are asleep, you will miss the ceromancy. Another factor is time. I value time like nothing more. I make sure every hour of my day adds value to my professional life, my personal life, or health. However, I am very selective about using my time wisely and with whom to spend it.

What is your favourite place in Oman, that you like to visit in order to relax and recharge your batteries?
I make sure I take a break when I need it. I go to the sea, wear my summer hat, and take my favourite book. And, of course, every few months, I go with my family to Jabal Akhdar to enjoy the fresh air.

Jokha Khalid Al Naamani

What was the best piece of advice that you were given regarding your career and that you will never forget?
"Never let anything stop you from achieving your goals and ambitions".

What has shaped you the most in your life? Is there any specific situation?
My passion for overcoming challenges is what shaped me the most. At the beginning of my career, one colleague in a high position made me feel like I could not succeed. So, I challenged myself using this situation as motivation; I worked hard and improved my work performance; surprisingly, within a few years, I reached his position.

Who would you identify as your role model? Whom do you look up to and why?
My father. He was a very hard-working man that was ambitious and had a futuristic view. He transformed his life from being a poor, unknown man to a successful, well-known businessman in Oman.

What do you respect most in other successful women?
I admire their strive for success in their personal lives and professional careers concurrently and their efforts towards achieving their goals.

What would you recommend to a student just starting and dreaming of a successful career?
Do not put limits on your ambitions, and always dream big. Keep working on yourself and improve your skills. Self-development is the best investment for your forthcoming years. Most importantly, aim for the stars, be sharp and focused, and do not turn to the competitors, thinking they will reach first. Mountain tops are not for one; they are for all.

What essential qualifications do you think will be needed ten years from now?
The world is moving towards digitalisation and programming; soon enough, artificial intelligence and smart tech will be the critical functions in managing day-to-day operations. Guiding our future generations towards entrepreneurship, building relationships, and communication is crucial. Presumably, their key future jobs would be marketing analysis, cyber securities, robots, user experience designing, and software development.

How would you describe your leadership style? What is your leadership motivation?
My primary leadership motivation is to see the best outcome in the worst situation and visualise it to create opportunities. I can classify my leadership style as a combination of coaching, innovative, and democratic styles. I can switch between the three styles to what I see fits the individual situation best.

If there is a lot of work and you are under stress, how do you compensate?
Prioritise tasks according to their urgency and importance.

Minister's advisor for information technology and statistics / Ministry of Labor

What are the three things in life you are most proud of?
I am proud of my success in my career; how I raised my children, I was overwhelmed when I found out that I was among the top 35 leaders of Oman.

Do you do anything to keep you fit physically or mentally, and how often?
Physically, walking outside four times a week. Moreover, I manage to stay mentally fit, nourishing my spirituality by practising my religion and attending coaching classes.

What does it take to be a successful woman these days? What are the three top things successful business people should personalise?
Courage, knowledge, and abandoning the fear of failure.

If you had extra time of four hours a day, what would you do during that time?
I would read more books, do more charity work, and give out coaching lessons to beginners.

What are your most important goals? Is there a difference for you between life goals and career goals?
By motivating myself and working hard, I achieved my main essential goals in both my personal life and career. As a result, I acquired the position I was striving for, and I am delighted with how I raised my children; and I can say that I live a luxurious life. Overall, I have achieved independence in all aspects of my life. My career and life goals are interlinked, so achieving one goal was like hitting two birds with one stone, which was very practical and satisfying.

Did the Omani culture you grew up in have an impact on your career path?
My parents strongly believed in equality between men and women. They encouraged me in my studies and held me responsible for my own life; this gave me independence in decision making, and as time passed, I became convinced that there is a solution to every problem.

What is your favourite place in Oman, that you like to visit in order to relax and recharge your batteries?
Salalah.

Kamilya Lamk Al-Lamki

What was the best piece of advice that you were given regarding your career and that you will never forget?
My mentor told me that I am a transformer as a teacher, not simply a disseminator of information. We help each child transform into their best version of themselves, so we will positively impact the lives of tens of thousands of students around the globe.

What would you recommend to a student just starting and dreaming of a successful career?
Your education is a gift; it will provide you with the tools necessary to make this world a better place. Your education, in every sense of the word, finds lessons from every event, every course, every interaction with people. Then, use those lessons to help and respect each other. Add in a dose of human kindness, and you have the recipe for a just and equitable future.

If the entire world listened to you for five minutes, what would you say or what would you want to talk about?
HONOR your intuition. Trust your gut and honour the message. You will make better decisions by valuing your intuition by not allowing the thoughts, feelings, or statements to take away from what you know to be true is very empowering.

- **GOALS.** Learn how to set personal and business purposes for yourself. Otherwise, it's like going aimlessly.
- **CONFIDENCE.** Believe in yourself, know your value, have something to say, and others will listen. Build the courage to speak your truth.
- **READ!** Books are an excellent resource to build your knowledge and expertise in any area.
- **YOUR HEALTH.** Eat right each day, fuelling your body with nutrients; you will feel better and have more energy. Exercise daily to take on the day with confidence because of how it makes you look and feel.
- **CHOOSE** Happiness. Content people are not held hostage by their circumstances but find reasons to be grateful. "Most people are about as happy as they make up their minds to be", Abraham Lincoln.
- **BUCKET LIST.** Start a bucket list with everything you want to achieve, do, see, feel, and experience in your life. When you invest in yourself, a world of opportunities will open for you. Know that no one will invest in you until you invest in yourself first.

How would you describe your leadership style? What is your leadership motivation?
Leading a school poised to engender lifelong learning, adaptability, and open communication; promote positive relationships among students, faculty, staff, and administrators; foster academic achievement; embrace diversity and respect for all. Building foundations for life success constitutes my ambition. In guiding my school, I promote and exercise a participatory leadership style where mutual decision making and collaboration is paramount. I believe in

Head of School / New World International School

creating an inspiring vision and mission statement exhibiting school values that need to be shared and supported within a well-structured organization, a favourable climate, and open communication.

Do you do anything to keep you fit physically or mentally, and how often?
I set a time every day for myself to concentrate on myself. It includes exercise, listening to music, reading inspirational and motivational documentaries on education and spending time with my most precious ones, especially my four amazing kids and my beloved soulmate, my husband. I like to reflect on what has happened and what I would like to manifest to happen. I have no regrets, and I choose to embrace all that I have and remain grateful.

What does it take to be a successful woman these days? What are the three top things successful business people should personalise?
Today's era is beginning to understand the importance of traditional ideals being carried on but not limiting anyone. We no longer need to promote values for a woman, such as femininity, modesty, discretion, virtue, and graciousness. Instead, the "ideal" woman can be anything she wants to be: glamorous, sophisticated, powerful, outspoken, career-minded, independent, self-sufficient, and sensual. She is in control of her own life, as well as the people and circumstances around her. Womanhood is a gift to be treasured, valued, and received with gratitude. We are wisely making an indelible mark on our communities, society, and future generations by our attitudes, words, and behaviour.

What would you devote your time and energy to if you were to invest now, in your future best self?
I would invest in self-love, as I cannot expect others to love me if I don't love myself. I am the only one who needs to take time to develop my gifts and talents to serve others best.

Is there a quote you favour that suits you? Or an important book you read that influenced you?
Remember, you are your own hero. The best version of yourself is your hero. Always aim to be your best version.

What are your most important goals? Is there a difference for you between life goals and career goals?
My life's goal is to become the best version of myself, seeing the best in others and helping them bring it out in themselves. I am here to make an impact. To ignite the spark of learning and to ensure it continues throughout their life. My goal is to enhance the quality of learning where the benefit is for the whole world by building a network that will facilitate changing the way learning happens.

Laila Al Hadhrami

What was the best piece of advice that you were given regarding your career and that you will never forget?
"Never underestimate your capabilities and don't keep working behind the stage" that advice was given by the best leader I ever worked with, my late General Manager Khalid Al Siyabi. His advice changed my life as I worked harder but not believing that I could be a leader and lead successful national projects later.

What has shaped you the most in your life? Is there any specific situation?
I still remember the day I left my family to study abroad. I was feeling excited to experience a new, mature life. I learned to fly and to manage my life expenses independently. That situation shaped my life to be independent and stronger, with self-confidence in my personality.

What do you respect most in other successful women?
'Empowering other women' is the essential element that I love to see with other female leaders. We should all keep supporting each other. Empowerment can be by teaching your skills to other women or coaching them to be more confident and believe in themselves.

What would you recommend to a student just starting and dreaming of a successful career?
Keep dreaming and believe that you will achieve your goals, but work harder to achieve measurable goals and not wait for others to give you a job. You are the one who can create your future.

If there is a lot of work and you are under stress, how do you compensate?
I reward myself with something that I love or make me happy because I deserve to celebrate the hard work I have achieved. I don't want others to reward me for my work because that

might not work; therefore, I keep rewarding myself to keep myself motivated and ready for other challenging tasks.

Do you do anything to keep you fit physically or mentally, and how often?
I give much attention to being fit mentally as the most important priority because it affects my productivity and physical fitness. In addition, being mentally fit makes me feel happy and optimistic. Therefore, I surround myself with optimistic people and avoid negative people.

What would you devote your time and energy to if you were to invest now, in your future best self?
I always believe that the best investment in ourselves is continuous self-learning. We should never stop learning, and we should have a written learning plan at the beginning of each year. For example, you might learn a new skill, learn a new language, experience a unique adventure, or even learn a new hobby. Every year, I write my goals and decide where I want to invest in myself for this year, and it might be linked to my career and personal goals.

Is there a quote you favour that suits you? Or an important book you read that influenced you?
"I Have a Dream" by Martin Luther King is one of my favourite phrases as it reminds me to keep dreaming and have a new achievable dream for each year. This phrase is one of the successful elements that pushes me to achieve my goals.

If you had extra time of four hours a day, what would you do during that time?
I would spend it reading and walking because reading is the most powerful tool for my mind, and walking is my favourite sport to clear the crowded ideas and think peacefully.

What are your most important goals? Is there a difference for you between life goals and career goals?
I always make sure to have a balance between my career goals and life goals. I work to achieve both of them by having a clear written KPI for each. Some people neglect life goals and focus only on career goals, which might affect their lives if they don't get the expected outcome. As a personal life goal, I learn new skills, read new books, and strive to achieve some dreams, like visiting all the countries worldwide. So far, I have seen over 50 countries, and I still have a long path.

What is your favourite place in Oman, that you like to visit in order to relax and recharge your batteries?
I have two favourite spots in Oman. First, I love beautiful, magical beaches and mountains in Oman. Jebel Akhdar (mountain) is my favourite spot running away from the heat of Muscat in the summer. We have a long, beautiful coast with breathtaking beaches. I feel blessed to have different climates with beautiful spots around Oman that make me fall in love with my beautiful country.

Laila Al Rawahi

Who would you identify as your role model? Whom do you look up to and why?
I feel deeply thankful to have had my mother as a role model. She inspired me with her altruism, work, and the positive contributions she made to the country and people. My mother was a Professor at Sultan Qaboos University and one of Oman's first appointed female members of the State Council. A loving, caring, and compassionate soul.

What do you respect most in other successful women?
Women who are unafraid to put forward their authentic selves, whether they choose to be stay-at-home mothers, caretakers of humanity, or work on a company board. This woman holds herself with dignity regardless of the job title she contains. A woman who is not fazed by conventional success stays true to her path, values, and beliefs. She competes with only herself. She has a strong appreciation for meritocracy and hard work. Her successes have been earned, and she is not afraid to speak up for what is right. She stands solid and calm in the face of any critics. Her goal is not to seek public accolades and applause but rather to elevate humanity discreetly and consistently.

What would you recommend to a student just starting and dreaming of a successful career?
Life is a journey, and we are all a by-product of our experiences. Give yourself time to understand yourself, look inward, and find what you are genuinely passionate about. Take the time to travel, visit different countries, talk to people you look up to, cultivate interests and hobbies, because only then will you truly discover where your passions are. Dream big, but know that anything genuine will take time, so be patient.

Do not give up on yourself when things get tough; belief in yourself and your dreams. Surround yourself with positive people and positive affirmations. The only thing you should worry about is your opinion of yourself, don't allow the opinions of others to influence your every move because that will only stifle your growth. Don't take life too seriously; choose your battles wisely, focus your energy on the matters and people that mean the most to you.

If the entire world listened to you for five minutes, what would you say or what would you want to talk about?
What if we woke up one morning and had a world with no borders? No countries or currencies define sovereignties or GDP metrics to list the richest to poorest countries, but instead, one planet we all belong to. Imagine, for just a moment, stripping away the politics and the egos and going back to the fundamental essence of what makes us all human. Every individual has compassion. Let us focus on our understanding and the badge of honour that guides us towards unity and cohesiveness.

If there is a lot of work and you are under stress, how do you compensate?
Everyone has their unique threshold; what might be stressful for one person could be the energy another person thrives on. The first step in managing stress levels is to understand your

Senior Business Finance Manager / HSBC

limitations. For example, I am typically my most productive in the morning, and my energy levels tend to dip in the afternoon. As such, I save the more cerebral work for the morning hours. Doing so allows me to manage my time, schedule calls, and prioritize accordingly. A crucial fact, which took me years to figure out, is that taking time off and unplugging is productive. I do yoga, and I make time to work out. It's one of the ways that I manage my stress levels. Maintaining a solid support group is also essential; my family keeps me grounded and helps me be the best version of myself. Grabbing a coffee with a family member or friend and having a laugh is one of the best remedies to a stressful day, as humour is healing.

Do you do anything to keep you fit physically or mentally, and how often?
I have been practising yoga for the past ten years. It helps me stay balanced and centred while also challenging me both mentally and physically. It is essential and healthy to have interests, passions, and hobbies outside of our work routines. It makes us happier and helps us perform better at work.

Is there a quote you favour that suits you? Or an important book you read that influenced you?
"Carpe Diem", meaning seize the moment. We live such fast-paced lives and forget to live in the moment. We should remember to make each day count and treat each day like the genuine gift it is.

How would you describe yourself in three words? Do you live with a daily routine, and what is your secret to success?
I realized that having a routine during the week is crucial to achieving my goals productively. After my early breakfast, some quiet time for me to reflect on my day ahead, followed by a workout (3 times a week). I then get ready for work. I usually have my calendar updated for the week early to balance out my time between work, myself, family, and friends. To describe me, I would use: I am adaptable, disciplined, and empathetic.

In my view, any success that I have derived mainly from my value system. If I were to define a formula for success, it would consist of pursuing the work that gives you meaning, waking up excited to start the day, knowing that you are bringing out the best in yourself and others. Instead, however, I focus on the quality of life, see family and friends, and have time for my own "self-care".

(Dr.) Laila Harub Al Kharusi

What was the best piece of advice that you were given regarding your career and that you will never forget?

I read this in an article as soon as I graduated from Uni. A nurse who worked in a hospice wrote it. She surveyed her terminally ill patients and asked them what their biggest regret in life was. Most of them said, "I regret wasting my time working more than living." This article shaped my entire philosophy when it came to working. I refused to be the slave of my career. I decided that I was to always work in a balanced manner. Until now, I haven't compromised on that, and I genuinely believe that I am succeeding quite well in my career because of it.

What has shaped you the most in your life? Is there any specific situation?

I believe my values, which I gather from my religion as a Muslim, and my father's disciplinarian ethos have a crucial role in shaping my life. On the other hand, the experiences that I went through, like becoming a dentist, becoming a wife, becoming a mother, becoming a manager, my ex-husband, my friends, and strangers, have all played a massive role in the person I am today. It was the accumulation of all the above that shaped me.

On the path to where you are now, what was the most determining step?

I don't recall ever making decisive steps. I am a typical Libran, so to say. I always look at the pros and cons of every situation, and I try to outweigh both ends, and I think about it, rethink, then rethink. It is sometimes exhausting how I can't decide because I don't want to do wrong by anyone. But, even becoming a chairperson in the Glocal Volunteering Organization and becoming the Managing Director of two of my father's dental clinic branches, all of that landed on my lap, and I took the challenge and went with it.

Who would you identify as your role model? Whom do you look up to and why?

I will have to name a few. To begin with the Prophet Mohd, for his perseverance in dealing with nomads and leading them, it takes a genius to do that. Princess Diana, for her beautiful soul and heart. Her unconditional love for the people. My father, for his way with people. A true diplomat at heart and, by far and without exaggeration, the most considerate person I have ever met on earth. My mother, for her patience and contentment in God - no one taught me that there is hope in hopelessness like she did.

What do you respect most in other successful women?

I respect the fact that they pushed through no matter society, culture, or whatever hurdle they had to jump over. They didn't give up, instead, they worked hard to be successful.

What would you recommend to a student just starting and dreaming of a successful career?

The world is your oyster. So, you be the writer of your story, don't let anyone else deprive you of your book cover.

Dentist / Harub Dental Surgery

If the entire world listened to you for five minutes, what would you say or what would you want to talk about?
I would not talk; in those 5 minutes, I would like to hear the world's priorities regarding poverty, famine, rape, and injustices. I would observe and listen. And after the 5 minutes were over, I would like to talk about why in the 21st century, we still have people dying because of these issues; some don't have water, food, aid, or education - basic human rights. Talking and venting won't change these circumstances; it needs to be mandatory for anyone to help and not just a gesture of kindness when one does.

What essential qualifications do you think will be needed ten years from now?
I think any qualification that is in the service of people will always be necessary. Like doctors, dentists, pharmacists, IT specialists, anything relevant to the benefit of people in a survival kind of way.

How would you describe your leadership style? What is your leadership motivation?
I like to listen and act quickly based on the advice given. I want to create a family-like environment but manage that at a level that clearly shows the red lines that can't be crossed. I am not complacent, nor do I entertain complacency in a workplace. I believe leadership is all about managing egos.

If there is a lot of work and you are under stress, how do you compensate?
I am the Goddess of Balance. I take a break for two days on a staycation, or I travel or get a massage. I believe taking care of myself is paramount to the thriving of my business.

What are your most important goals? Is there a difference for you between life goals and career goals?
Someone once told me, "Love what you are doing so that you can do what you love". I love dentistry and running the family dental practice, so that is my purpose now, to be of service to my patients and the public. But my dream on a bigger scale is to do volunteering around the world. I want to be more purposeful and to serve the people on a bigger scale.

Lamia Al Ansi

What was the best piece of advice that you were given regarding your career and that you will never forget?
"Ensure you do the right and transparent thing. You are untouchable if you just do that". That one sentence from a senior in the governance helped me always be at peace when presented with conflicting objectives. You can always pose your views if they are based on win-win, transparency, and logic.

On the path to where you are now, what was the most determining step?
My most decisive step was finding that following my heart has served me well, even when my brain doesn't get it. For example, when I changed jobs, it felt odd to those around me to leave secure positions where I am recognised and supported, to try to establish my space all over again. However, this granted me broadening, context, and a broader perspective, as well as a continuous chance to challenge myself and my comfort zone.

What do you respect most in other successful women?
I always admire how successful women can balance their caregiver side (mothers, sisters, wives) with balancing an ever-growing complex work environment. There is not enough time in the day, yet some women manage it with grace and diligence in such an admirable manner. I also admire the empathy and support systems provided by female networks. When done right, it liberates the energy of unmatched potential.

What essential qualifications do you think will be needed ten years from now?
Resilience and innovative decision making, accelerated learning, coding, presentation, negotiations, as well as data presentation.

How would you describe your leadership style? What is your leadership motivation?
Inclusive leadership, where my motivation is being surrounded by the best and bringing out the best in them. My conviction is that authentic leadership is not you knowing everything; you need to know enough to probe, but true and powerful leadership motivates and moves others to be the best versions of themselves towards a common and impactful goal.

If there is a lot of work and you are under stress, how do you compensate?
I opt for physical and nature-related activities. Discipline is critical in today's disruptive world.

Head Special Projects / PDO and Board Director / Oman Development Bank

What works for me is a reminder of our humanity in a disciplined and scheduled manner: I work out and prefer outdoor workouts when I can, such as hikes, biking, swims, and simple walks.

What does it take to be a successful woman these days? What are the three top things successful business people should personalise?
To be successful, be yourself. We all have our innate natural strengths, and I find we shall focus on our strengths (rather than improving weaknesses). The second important thing is to remember that the voice you have matters; speak up even if your inner self is hesitant- you bring diversity and new perspective to the table, so do not hold yourself from offering that in the decision-making process. Finally, take care of yourself. We tend to work hard and set high standards for ourselves and others, which is excellent sometimes, but many times, you need to draw the line where you are taking on board more than you should. Do not be tough on yourself and learn to accept that sometimes you need to allow others to deliver.

What would you devote your time and energy to if you were to invest now, in your future best self?
I would put my time and energy into understanding myself deeper. For example, what are my core values, what purpose I serve in life, and how can I spend more time on activities that fulfil that purpose. I think, in a way, I am 75% there- but if I could, I would dedicate more time to it.

If you had extra time of four hours a day, what would you do during that time?
I would explore and travel! I was reflecting the other day on how I have mastered the whole working from recent home developments, whereby I can log in from different spots and enjoy the new areas after work.

What are your most important goals? Is there a difference for you between life goals and career goals?
I want to always be content, happy and free. Work, life, leisure- it is all life, and I would not compromise in any aspect of the big picture.

Did the Omani culture you grew up in have an impact on your career path?
Oman is a mosaic of cultures, which are magnificent and rich. I am lucky to have come from parents who represent different regions and cultures and been raised in the post-1970's era, which introduced a new Oman. I am more and more proud of our down to earth, practical and naturally environmental culture. Professionally, it shapes which entities I want to be associated with. I think that is why I am always gravitating towards entities with a broader social impact.

What is your favourite place in Oman, that you like to visit in order to relax and recharge your batteries?
Salalah. It smells special; it feels special, and I love the food and the vibes. Overall, in Oman, go out of the standard path and walk in the alleyways and small corner shops; you will always discover a surprising and fantastic find.

Lamya Adnan Al Haj

What was the best piece of advice that you were given regarding your career and that you will never forget?
My brother introduced me to the 80/20 Pareto principle. It helps me focus on 20% of the necessary actions that give you 80% of the results. It gives you that momentum of working intelligently rather than working hard. Another excellent piece of advice came from my mum. She always said, "Don't wait for thanks from anyone", and she always reminded me, "The only person you should compete with is yourself!"

What has shaped you the most in your life? Is there any specific situation?
Due to my 'perfectionist personality', I used to have a lot of anxiety, which was sometimes an obstacle. With time, I learned how to deal with very stressful situations and overcome them, making me a stronger person, and it helped shape my personality. I realised that I developed and evolved as a person with the obstacles in my life, and I thank Allah for every experience I went through. I truly believe in the statement, "What doesn't kill you makes you stronger."

Who would you identify as your role model? Whom do you look up to and why?
I have several role models for different aspects of life. My dad inspired me in the field of academia and high achievements. He was a professor and pushed us to achieve well. My mom is my role model of parenting and inactive social work. That is where I got my social work passion. My husband was a role model in perseverance, sacrifice and support, while my siblings motivated me in professional development. The late Sh. Khalfan Al Asari and my elder brother are my role models in leadership and empowerment.

What would you recommend to a student just starting and dreaming of a successful career?
Find your way. Find your why. The earlier you find your why, the faster you can follow your passion. There's a practice called the Ikigai, which is a Japanese concept of happiness. It's a practical exercise that asks you a set of questions that dive deep into a person's emotions where you discover your why. Follow your passion, and nothing will stop you.

Associate Professor of Molecular Biology / Sultan Qaboos University
Founder & CEO / Coach4Change

If the entire world listened to you for five minutes, what would you say or what would you want to talk about?
Respect, Love, support, and empower one another. Yes, I would focus my talk on the importance of peace, caring, sharing, supporting and empowering each other. Try to empower and help as many people as you can along your way. Be kind, spread joy and happiness around you and always leave the place you are in, in a better condition. Give and do not wait for thanks from anyone; change people's life. Love for others what you love for yourself. That is when the world is going to change and become a better place!

What essential qualifications do you think will be needed ten years from now?
CEO, but a different kind of CEO, a chief emotional officer. I believe that resilience and having a very high emotional intelligence are significant because they help you solve problems and be a better collaborator and communicator. You can do wonders with a high EQ!

How would you describe your leadership style? What is your leadership motivation?
I would describe my leadership style as 'horizontal leadership'. I am a 'Multiplier!' I believe in engagement, team spirit, motivation, raising together, and creating more leaders along the way. I am not fond of vertical leadership. I ensure that each member of my team feels equally important just in different ways, and I constantly remind them that we all work toward the same goal. I try to use the power of 'emotional intelligence' as it brings the best out of people and unleashes potential. I enjoy leadership because it allows me to empower and raise people around me.

Which topics should humanity focus more on in the future?
Well, I would say technologies on the technical skills side and emotional and social intelligence on the soft skills side. It is becoming vital for people's mental health, survival and general happiness. Important technical subjects are artificial intelligence and robotics. We're shifting to an artificial intelligence world with cybersecurity and blockchain technology.

Is there a quote you favour that suits you? Or an important book you read that influenced you?
I love Gandhi's quote, "Be the change you want to see in the world". I strongly believe in it, live by it, practise and teach it. When you believe you can change the world into a better place, it gives you a great reason to live, which is the core of our Islamic teachings. It is a true motivation.

What are your most important goals? Is there a difference for you between life goals and career goals?
One of my favourite and most important goals is to empower others, specifically the Arab youth and empower the poor. I have worked with refugees and the less advantaged for years. I've travelled to several places outside Oman to support refugees, help them in their education and sustainable lifestyle as much as I can with my limited resources. But I like to make a bigger difference in the world around me.

(Dr.) Lamya Harub

Who would you identify as your role model? Whom do you look up to and why?
I would say the bookstores. Aside from people that have influenced me, many authors have been my inspiration. I have learned a lot about life from reading writers like Said, Mitchell, Murakami, Freud, Roy, Khalfan and Plato. My understanding of life comes from several distinct characters in books. Reading has allowed me to have multiple role models, all of which change with time and context.

What do you respect most in other successful women?
When a woman does not allow the social construct of gender to become an obstacle in everything she does, I respect her. We are more than a "gender", and I refuse to be limited in that way.

What would you recommend to a student just starting and dreaming of a successful career?
To find alternative realities, one must yield to the arts. Here I mean all arts, like drama, poetry, fiction, cinema, and television. There is an instinct in the human mind to find stories and alternative fantasies and experiment with reality. Because we need alternative facts, our mind produces them. I believe that when we submit to and express ourselves in the arts, our dreams of success (in life) follow.

How would you describe your leadership style? What is your leadership motivation?
Leadership is about being optimistic. Being optimistic, one can envision a better future for the organisation, the country, and the workforce. With optimism, leaders can inspire and motivate people to work toward achieving a shared vision of success.

Which topics should humanity focus more on in the future?
Climate change. Today, communities are already facing more extreme and frequent droughts, floods, and other weather events. These consequences will only intensify if global temperatures exceed the two-degree ceiling. Moreover, adaptation costs could reach double the worst-case figures, placing a crippling burden on the world economy. Given that everyone will be responsible for adjustment, Oman (and the world leaders) needs to prioritise climate change.

Is there a quote you favour that suits you? Or an important book you read that influenced you?
The post-structuralist philosopher, Jacques Derrida, said: "The circle of the return to birth can only remain open, but this is a chance, a sign of life, and a wound." Of course, my understanding of this quote may differ from his articulation of it. Nonetheless, I am moved by the selection, as it allows me to see things from infinite perspectives. Cheerful as it may sound, but challenging as well when discoursing with binary-minded individuals.

What are your most important goals?
Is there a difference for you between life
goals and career goals?
I do not draw dichotomies between my life
at work or home. My goal does not fluctuate
in a different context. I believe in creating
meaningfulness in every step I take. I am trying to embed meaningfulness in every word,
action, performance, or discourse that I am
engaged in.

Did the Omani culture you grew up in have
an impact on your career path?
Growing up in Oman has allowed me to have
a unique view of the interactions between
different cultures. The Sultanate's diverse
landscape and multi-cultural history define
in many ways the meaning of the culture
construct, i.e., the mixing of things from
various sources. This is evident in the way we
live and work, where the so-called 'East' and
'West' come together gracefully, influencing
our daily endeavours.

What is your favourite place in Oman,
that you like to visit in order to relax and
recharge your batteries?
The mountains of Jebel Al Akhdar, the waves
of Salalah, the Dam of Wadi Dayqah, the
blossoms of Wakan Village, the vastness of
Jebel Al Abyad in Al Sharqiya, the Turtle
reserves in Ras al-Jinz, are the list of many
locations I choose to repose in.

Lujaina Al Kharusi

What has shaped you the most in your life? Is there any specific situation?
Many of the experiences I faced throughout my journey have shaped me. My childhood, the experiences I went through in school, and the people I met in my life. I don't think it's simple to pinpoint a particular situation or experience. I also believe it stems from the values we carry and have been taught. Good experiences allow us to amplify these values and unpleasant experiences allow us to stick to our values.

On the path to where you are now, what was the most determining step?
Being my authentic self. It is easy when we are starting our own family, climbing the career ladder or working on achieving success to do things for the sake of impressing or pleasing others, even if it does not fit with our values. We can lose our voice and ourselves. Throughout, I have learned that to live a happy and content life is to be my authentic self.

Who would you identify as your role model? Whom do you look up to and why?
I don't have a particular role model. Any man, woman, or even a child who has enlightened me or inspired me in one form or another is a role model. But, in general, I am always touched by people who live an authentic life, and I look up to confident people without arrogance. I like people who are always giving without expecting a return.

What do you respect most in other successful women?
I always considered the word success very subjective, as it means different things to different people. For me, I respect a successful woman who is very confident and able to achieve her goals in the most authentic way. Furthermore, I appreciate a woman who does not need to pretend or get the approval of others to reach her goals.

What would you recommend to a student just starting and dreaming of a successful career?
First, I would advise any student to be a good listener and observer. To take in the dynamics of the real world and understand how it works. To always seek information and, most impor-

Head of Regulatory and Corporate Affairs / Vodafone Oman
Entrepreneur, Investor & Business Coach

tantly, to build relationships based on respect and support. For women, in particular, my advice is to always be comfortable with who you are and understand that you bring something unique to the business or career world that complements men as a woman. Don't try to be something you are not. Embrace who you are and trust that it's your strength.

If the entire world listened to you for five minutes, what would you say or what would you want to talk about?
I think it would be about choice and freedom. I believe many people struggle (including myself sometimes) in understanding that we have the freedom to choose what we want to be and do in life. We believe we must do certain things a certain way; otherwise, we won't survive. I will want to talk more about how conforming to people's way, beliefs, culture, and even jobs are more painful and more complicated than being fearless and making our own choices in life.

If there is a lot of work and you are under stress, how do you compensate?
With all honesty, I do nothing. Instead, I take time to relax and be at home with my family. I love being at home and spending time watching TV.

Do you do anything to keep you fit physically or mentally, and how often?
I try to play tennis at least once a week, journal and meditate daily. I'd love to do more, though, and be more consistent.

Which topics should humanity focus more on in the future?
I would name inclusion and mental health. Especially in these times where the world is more divided, people have no tolerance for each other. This should change.

If you had extra time of four hours a day, what would you do during that time?
Along with my full-time job and four kids, I am also a businesswoman, so an extra 4 hours a day would be incredible. I'll divide them equally between family time and my business goals.

Did the Omani culture you grew up in have an impact on your career path?
I would say no. I think it is more a personality thing than a culture. The environment we live in can make it easier or complex, but our personality determines our path.

What is your favourite place in Oman, that you like to visit in order to relax and recharge your batteries?
I have many favourite places! We are blessed with such a beautiful country that allows us to disconnect and enjoy nature. One of my favourite places I have visited is a village 2000 meters above sea called Wakan. The hike there is just out of this world.

Honorable
Lujaina Mohsin Darwish (FRSA)

What was the best piece of advice that you were given regarding your career and that you will never forget?
This advice came from my father, who was always a firm believer in teamwork. He always told me that if we care for our employees, they, in turn, will take care of the business. This is a golden truth that I have tried to follow each day of my work life and will continue to do so.

Whom would you name is your role model - whom do you look up to? Why?
My late father has been the role model that I have always looked up to my entire life. He taught me the most valuable life lessons, which have made me what I am today. The values he inculcated in me continue to guide me every day of my life. He always encouraged me to grow up into a strong individual and create a distinct identity for myself. He was the mentor who has always been by my side, guiding and encouraging me to face newer challenges. He will always be my inspiration.

What do you respect most in other successful women?
There are so many qualities that I admire with the incredible women who have always inspired me. The resilience to pursue their dreams, overcome social and economic challenges and not give up mid-way. The grit and the tenacity to stay focused on their goals and learn from failures. This fraternity keeps making me proud every day; I feel enlightened, inspired, and empowered in their company.

If the whole world listened to you for 5 minutes, what would you say or what would you want to talk about?
I would tell them two critical things.
Firstly, to everyone, women are the most precious gifts to humanity. They are the ones who will continue to shape societies all over the world. Secondly, to women, have a joyous listen to your inner self. Then, if you have faith and conviction, you can make things happen.

How would you describe your leadership style? What is your leadership motivation?
I have always believed in the power of inclusivity and collective thought.
My management mantra has been to empower employees, include them in the decision-making process. This makes them feel empowered to contribute and think freely.

If there is a lot of work and you are stressed - how do you compensate?
I usually read books. It helps me relax and shift focus. I also indulge in gardening and being

Chairperson - ITICS / Mohsin Haider Darwish LLC &
State Council Member | Board Member / Oman Football Association

amid nature, which helps me unwind and recharge. I think nature can heal like nothing else. I also go for walks along the beach. It helps me stay fit and energised.

Which topics should humanity focus more on in the future?
Education that is relevant to the future is one of the most pressing issues. We have to ramp up the quality of education taught to children and see how it can be aligned to the demands of the 4th industrial revolution. Technical know-how is mandatory and needs to be imbibed from a young age. Only then we will be able to align ourselves with the deliverables of the Oman Vision 2040.

What does it take to be a successful woman these days? What are the three top things successful business people should personalise?
There are quite a few pieces of advice that have helped me become what I am today. But if I were to shortlist the top three, it would be these: Efficient time management; multitasking is a given in today's time. If we don't manage time well, nothing else will work. Identifying the best people and resources who can deliver. Recognising the hard work of people who have given results and motivating the ones who can do better.

If you had extra time of four hours a day, what would you do during that time?
It would be wonderful to have additional few hours every day. I would love to have more time to mentor and guide entrepreneurs on being successful and staying focused on their dream goals. I feel that SME's are the building blocks for the economy of the country, and as established businesses, we have to help these young entrepreneurs grow and prosper.

What are your most important goals? Is there a difference for you between life goals and career goals?
The most important goal should be to become a better human being. This is something that my father always advised. If we work towards this goal single-mindedly, all other dreams will automatically be realised.

Does the Omani culture you grew up in have an impact on your career path?
Absolutely. Oman is one of the most diverse and beautiful countries in the world. The Omani society is tolerant, inclusive and far-sighted. Everyone across the globe admires the renowned hospitable nature of Omanis. I have been fortunate enough to have been given the correct values of respect and compassion for human beings irrespective of gender, ethnicity or origin.

What is your favourite place in Oman, that you like to visit in order to relax and recharge your batteries?
Oman is blessed with a splendid coastline. I love taking long walks along the beach. The ocean waves gently hugging the sands are a magical experience. It makes me realise each day that we human beings are so minuscule in front of the mighty nature. It is a humbling experience. But, it helps me stay grounded and come back refreshed to work.

Maani Abdullah Hamed Al Busaidi

What was the best piece of advice that you were given regarding your career and that you will never forget?
Take people for their strengths. Each individual is unique, and we need to focus on these positive aspects.

What do you respect most in other successful women?
I respect other successful women's self-esteem in their ability to multitask and knowing that they can tackle any situation no matter what.

What would you recommend to a student just starting and dreaming of a successful career?
As a young student, you should have faith in yourself and know that you can succeed no matter what obstacle you are faced with. I would conclude by using the quote, "Winners never quit, and quitters never win."

If the entire world listened to you for five minutes, what would you say or what would you want to talk about?
I would let my audience know that life is not a bed of roses. The thorns in the rose's stem may hurt. Because of this experience, life teaches us that we have to accept that there are happy and sentimental situations and sad ones. We should try to always focus on the good aspects and never give up.

How would you describe your leadership style? What is your leadership motivation?
A true leader can delegate the work accordingly with a high-end result in which each individual sees their effort through teamwork.

If there is a lot of work and you are under stress, how do you compensate?
I would take a break, and sometimes I listen to music that I enjoy.

What are the three things in life you are most proud of?
The three attributes that I hold close to my heart are my inner circle of the family. Second, my achievements are my backbone. And third, I am proud of my coaching style on the work front.

Director General of Family Development /
Ministry of Social Development in Sultanate of Oman

Do you do anything to keep you fit physically or mentally, and how often?
The health benefits of everyday activity are essential, as it's known.

Still, it's challenging for me to do exercises because of my busy schedule during the day, so I keep my body fit by not having any meals from 6 PM till 8 AM during the weekdays.

What does it take to be a successful woman these days? What are the three top things successful business people should personalise?
To be a successful woman in today's world means having faith and believing what you are doing is right. Honesty no matter what, integrity, and confidence.

If you had extra time of four hours a day, what would you do during that time?
I would enjoy the added time by spending it with my family and watching a movie.

How would you describe yourself in three words what is your secret to success?
I'm dynamic, unique, and straightforward.

What is your favourite place in Oman, that you like to visit in order to relax and recharge your batteries?
Oman is known for its beautiful and pristine beaches. I enjoy going to the beach with my cup of coffee to relax and unwind. The peace of the humming of the birds and the sound of the waves provides me with inner tranquillity.

Maha Al Balushi

What was the best piece of advice that you were given regarding your career and that you will never forget?
Please don't wait for people to appreciate your achievements and reward you. Instead, be proactive, ask for what you deserve explicitly and fight for it till you get it.

What has shaped you the most in your life? Is there any specific situation?
I have been exposed to different cultures since I was a child. This built many values in me, such as accepting people the way they are, respecting their differences, and having inner peace and stability. Studying abroad was a broad experience from all perspectives.

On the path to where you are now, what was the most determining step?
The first time I changed my working place! It was difficult for me emotionally to leave the centre that I built from scratch, all my friends and the excellent working environment for a new adventure. However, I realised later that it was a right and healthy decision. It opened my horizons to new experiences, knowledge, and opportunities.

What would you recommend to a student just starting and dreaming of a successful career?
You have to understand every element of the ecosystem surrounding your industry or, more specifically, your daily work. To do that, you have to work hard and try doing different tasks. It will sharpen your skills and expand your connections, which are essential for a successful career. In contrast, you need to stay focused and not distract your career path unless you find your passion for something else through this exploration journey! Of course, all of that would mean extra working hours.

If the entire world listened to you for five minutes, what would you say or what would you want to talk about?
I would talk about peace! Open your mind and heart, attach yourself to nothing, and please go back to your humanity. We have to believe in it and find it within ourselves first, and then we can start to fix the world.

How would you describe your leadership style? What is your leadership motivation?
Leadership is a combination of art and science. I believe in giving my team members the space to innovate by delegating tasks, supervise, support and interfere only when necessary. Of course, this happens gradually after knowing them very well and understanding their skill sets and personalities. I need to gain their trust and loyalty. My leadership motivation is to have a positive impact on my team members. I push them to develop their skills, love and enjoy what they do, just like myself, through providing a healthy and supportive working environment.

If there is a lot of work and you are under stress, how do you compensate?
My immediate and first plan for stress relief is hiking. It helps a lot to vent out all work and life stress. Luckily, Oman is full of varieties for hiking! First, it is gorgeous, especially in

wintertime. Second, I would go for a weekend out of the city and come fresh and ready for more work and challenges.

What are the three things in life you are most proud of?
My wonderful and supportive family. My achievements in my career and academic path. In May 2018, I received an award from the Gov. of Oman represented in the Ministry of Transport, Communication and Information Technology for all my efforts to establish the ICT entrepreneurial ecosystem in Oman. The positive impact on my start-ups' companies on a personal and professional level. Inspiring people and being part of their success and learning curve is a very satisfying feeling. It is the best reward that a practitioner can receive.

Do you do anything to keep you fit physically or mentally, and how often?
I exercise daily. In the hectic weeks, I exercise a minimum of three times a week. Usually, I go hiking or walking. Currently, I am planning to explore new sports such as horse riding and yoga. Sport is one of the best ways to vent out all stress and muscle stiffness caused by sitting for long hours at work.

What would you devote your time and energy to if you were to invest now, in your future best self?
I will focus on up-scaling some current skills and building up some more specialised technical training courses in these skills. I will read more in relevant areas. In addition, I will plan for my future business ideas more seriously.

How would you describe yourself in three words? Do you live with a daily routine?
Yes, and no! Yes, because it is the same flow of activities every day. Yet, no, because every day is different. Working with start-ups is an endless drama. Every day there are new challenges that make my day dynamic. We discuss, negotiate, and find solutions to resolve them. Success comes with a combination of many elements, if I would name the three most important reasons, in my opinion, confidence, maturity and flexibility.

What is your favourite place in Oman, that you like to visit in order to relax and recharge your batteries?
Oman is blessed with many places perfect for relaxation and recharging batteries. I love Musandam a lot. Exceptional beaches with clear waters and incredible dolphins accompanying you in an unfair race in sea tour.

Maha Saud Kalmoor Al Raisi

On the path to where you are now, what was the most determining step?
One decision can change life for a brighter future. We often get so caught up in the desire to make the right decision that we end up not deciding at all. Therefore, it was vital for me to move out of my comfort zone. One such decision was to move to Doha, Qatar, gain some regional exposure, widen my knowledge, and work in different cultures and environments. Personally and professionally, it turned out to be successful.

What would you recommend to a student just starting and dreaming of a successful career?
Be bold and daring, be ready to accept failures as that is the only way you can learn, be open to any criticism you receive to help shape your personality and never give up. Every success comes with a little bit of sacrifice, and it is up to us to dictate how much we are willing to sacrifice. Being successful in your career does not mean that you would fail as a mother or parent. You need to know how to multitask. You have to take hold of your life and not wait for the opportunities to come, but you need to grab them.

What essential qualifications do you think will be needed ten years from now?
The world is changing every day and what was accurate about a decade ago is not relevant today. I see tech skills in high demand, expertise around various software programs, platforms, systems, and services; soft skills will remain suitable as robots will take much time to be as emotionally intelligent as people. Virtual reality is here to stay.

If there is a lot of work and you are under stress, how do you compensate?
I enjoy taking care of my garden and spending quality time nurturing, being with nature. It brings a sense of calmness, which is extremely important to develop a positive state of mind. I also enjoy sitting and chatting with my youngest girl, who makes me forget the world around me. In addition, I enjoy long drives, road trips and absorbing the nature and scenic beauty that my country presents in abundance.

What are the three things in life you are most proud of?
I value all my relationships and acquaintances over the years, and each of them has impacted what I am today. I am proud of how I have been able to raise my children. Each of my seven

Head of Retail Products / National Bank of Oman

kids is developing to be a good human being. I am proud of the way I have been able to support my family financially and emotionally. Last but not least, I am proud of my professional position; I realised that all the efforts, sacrifices, and sweat seem to pay off.

Which topics should humanity focus more on in the future?
"Rolling stones never gather moss" is an often-used adage. We need to keep evolving and moving every day. Never stop learning, as that is the only way we can progress as individuals and as humankind. I don't want to be prescriptive or be limited to a topic but explore every opportunity to learn something new every day.

What does it take to be a successful woman these days? What are the three top things successful business people should personalise?
Irrespective of gender, one needs to be inclusive to succeed in any field, personal or professional. Business people need to be energetic and motivated, willing to listen, and determined to succeed. What would you devote your time and energy to if you were to invest now, in your future best self? I would do more reading and work with aspiring children, especially girls, and teach them the importance of being educated, aspirational and driven.

If you had extra time of four hours a day, what would you do during that time?
In addition to spending some more quality time with my family, especially kids, sharing my goals, aspirations, learnings, I would also like to read more and keep myself in the process of being updated on the changes that are more dynamic than ever.

Do you live with a daily routine?
It isn't easy to juggle as a mother, wife, daughter, and ambitious career woman every day. However, if I don't plan and prepare myself and set a 'routine', I will never be able to do justice to the multiple roles required to perform. I am thankful to my family, who follows what I think is best for them and makes it work.

Did the Omani culture you grew up in have an impact on your career path?
Suppose you examine the dynamic role of women in the Sultanate of Oman; you will observe that women not only remain the backbone of societal continuity but have contributed to the development of this country in its ambition to be a modern, stable and optimistic state as it is today.

What is your favourite place in Oman, that you like to visit in order to relax and recharge your batteries?
Oman has breathtaking landscapes, mountain ranges, historic forts, warm beaches, and destinations. I love visiting Misfat Al Abriyeen, which captures the traditional atmosphere of mountain life, Bahla, located in Northern Oman and is a kind of oasis in the desert and Salalah. This coastal region has transformed into a green oasis with seasonal waterfalls and streams.

Maimuna Al-Sulaimani

Whom would you name is your role model - whom do you look up to? Why?
His Majesty Late Sultan Qaboos, may he rest in peace. He is such a Historical Global leader.
I belong to a generation His Majesty created by establishing education and fantastic opportunities to study abroad via high standard scholarships. My generation is so lucky and shall stay committed to paying back by keeping His Majesty's values and legacy.

What would you recommend a student just starting and dreaming of a successful career?
Understand and embrace a professional mentor; it's your lifetime career secure base.

What essential qualifications do you think will be needed ten years from now?
Human Resources are treasures. It is fundamental to create a robust framework that allows vocational training, licensing, regulation and accountability. This is expected to ensure compliance to ethics, mentoring, and fair chances to all based on clear and transparent criteria.

How would you describe your leadership style? What is your leadership motivation?
As an educator and academic, I consider my leadership style of a Consultative Leader. I enjoy knowledge transfer and allow others to interpret the ideas and arrive at innovative outcomes and build an enlightened young generation with high calibre. I love and enjoy meeting students and developing their critical thinking and debate skills.

What are the three things in your life you are most proud of?
My career path and being appointed by His Majesty Late Sultan Qaboos as a Commissioner in the Omani Human Rights Committee 2019-2022, my children, and establishing the Law & Life Project. I found Law & Life 10 years ago. Now, Law & Life is a well-known project in my society. We succeeded in Launching one of a kind Bilingual Legal Magazine, organising an annual Omani Law Conference, introduced a legal apprenticeship program to train young lawyers, and finally and most recently, opened the first Omani Law Library licensed since 2017.

Do you do anything to keep you fit – physically or mentally, and how often do you do that?
Apart from short breaks after significant achievements, I ensure daily mental reflection, reading and meditation. This routine is so important to continue what I do and serve others further. Regular weekly physical fitness with my personal trainer is a priority as well.

What does it take to be a successful woman these days? What are the three top things successful business people should personalise?
I believe that success is gender-neutral. Having said that, a successful person's mindset should avoid gender bias. One should strike a balance between his authenticity on the one hand and serving the larger society on the other hand. Additionally, dedicating time to contribute to

Omani Human Rights Commission Member | Founder of Law& Life | Supreme Court Licensed Law Firm (L.L.M.)

building a balanced and seasoned character is important. A successful individual is open-minded and benchmarks their level to International Professional standards. Finally, in my opinion, one should focus and invest in building a genuine network, ethics and apply Rule of Law.

If you had extra time of four hours a day, what would you do during that time?
Spend more extended time with my mother and dedicate time to recording her interesting life stories so I can publish a book about her inspiring life experience of a wise Omani woman and true survivor journey. I always have time to conduct more workshops on legal awareness to ensure equal access to Omani laws to various segments of the Omani society. Further time I would spend in legal research for legal alerts to my audience and draft more books!

Are you living within a daily routine? How would you describe yourself in three words? What is your secret to success?
I have a hybrid approach, as while my team prepares a weekly and monthly schedule, I'm flexible during the working hours since the nature of my work as a lawyer is to serve people and expect surprises. Furthermore, my routine as a legal counsel starts after working hours, where I spend quiet time drafting opinions while my kids do homework. Finally, I appreciate my digital presence and meeting minds over ideas and intellectual discussions over various new media platforms such as Twitter, Linked In, and Snapchat.

I would describe myself in three words: enthusiastic, multi-tasking and considering.
The secret to my success is believing that the best is not yet to come, but we create it, allow people to subscribe to it, and allow it to manifest.

Does the Omani culture you grew up in have an impact on your career path?
Like many Omani families, I'm proud to come from a family that embrace gender and differences. I was brought up in a large extended family.

By the time I was 17 years old and ready to travel for my Scholarship to study Law, I remember my cousin who is 8 years older than me telling me, Maimuna, make the best out of the crowd you are coming from. By now, you have developed high skills in Emotional Intelligence and Resilience, make use of them!

Maisa Al Hooti

What has shaped you the most in your life? Is there any specific situation?
I remember having a conversation with someone shortly after I had graduated high school. I was asked what I was planning to study, and I replied, 'photography'. This person then advised me to specialise in underwater photography. Initially, I objected because I had a phobia of the deep sea. However, I then decided that I would challenge myself and overcome my fears. As a result, I got my diving qualifications and then started specialising in the field that is now my passion.

On the path to where you are now, what was the most determining step?
At a very young age, I decided I would constantly challenge myself and pursue big dreams. But the most decisive step was when I decided to face my fear of diving, which led me to do what I am doing today; namely, underwater photography and I enjoy every minute of it.

Who would you identify as your role model? Whom do you look up to and why?
My mother is my greatest inspiration. She is always ready to listen to her children and give good advice. My siblings and I always knew that we had a reliable friend and a confident guide growing up. She has worked hard to make our home a place of safety and serenity. She has also shown us how to be successful in business by being a good example herself.

What do you respect most in other successful women?
I respect women who professionally approach their work and take responsibility for what they do. However, this should be in a manner that reflects our nature as women, as we have the power to use gentleness and love to guide and lead others in the right direction, without forgetting our culture and heritage.

If the entire world listened to you for five minutes, what would you say or what would you want to talk about?
Being a proud Omani woman, I am always looking for opportunities to tell the world how wonderful our country is. We have such a rich culture and diverse and beautiful landscapes, and the nature of Omani people is known for their hospitality and kindness. So I am always encouraging people to visit Oman and experience the beauty of the Sultanate for themselves.

How would you describe your leadership style? What is your leadership motivation?
In my company, I have carefully chosen a team of people that I can trust and who can take the initiative when they need to. I believe that people work best when they are given the freedom to express themselves and learn and grow their skills. However, I believe in leading by example, and I am always at their side to give them hands-on guidance.

If there is a lot of work and you are under stress, how do you compensate?
I like to stay in touch with my friends and family, who are my support structure. However, I know I can always rely on my mother to guide me when I need it.

Which topics should humanity focus more on in the future?
Even though there has been a recent shift in public discourse concerning the conservation of the environment, I still think there is a lot to be done. As an activist for marine conservation, I hope to spend a lot more time and resources on preserving our world's oceans.

What does it take to be a successful woman these days?
To be a successful businesswoman requires a lot of perseverance, diligence, and patience. A successful person has kept on going when others have given up. I also believe that any job worth doing is worth doing well, setting you apart from others. One should also be patient with others, but mostly with oneself. In this life, we are constantly developing, so give yourself time to grow into the person you want to become.

What would you devote your time and energy to if you were to invest now, in your future best self?
I am always thinking ahead about where I want to be in two years, five years and ten years. So I like to find out as much as possible about new developments and techniques in my industry. I also spend time cultivating good, solid relationships with other businesswomen. This is because I recognise that we can benefit from supporting one another and learning from each other.

Did the Omani culture you grew up in have an impact on your career path?
Yes. I am very proud to be an Omani, and I always aspire to follow Omani values in my work. I have also made it my goal to share the beauty and wonders of Oman with the world.

What is your favourite place in Oman, that you like to visit in order to relax and recharge your batteries?
I love diving at Daymaniyat Islands. There is such a wealth of marine life living in the surrounding corals. If I could, I would go there every day. I love being underwater and experiencing the beauty of the ocean, exploring areas that I never dreamed I would go to.

Majan Al Abdullatif

What was the best piece of advice that you were given regarding your career and that you will never forget?
One of my managers advised me to ensure that I am clear on the intent when asking a question (e.g., the purpose of my question is, or I am asking this because...). I have found that you can build trust and credibility by ensuring an explicit statement of intent. Not everyone expects that, and it puts them at ease to discuss various topics.

On the path to where you are now, what was the most determining step?
Being open to various opportunities earlier in my career, and more specifically as I grew and developed.

Who would you identify as your role model? Whom do you look up to and why?
My Husband. He has been my partner throughout, my sounding board, sense of reality and also stretched me to dream. It has made a massive difference to my life knowing I have someone I can speak to about everything and anything and that he will always have my best interest at heart and support me.

What do you respect most in other successful women?
I highly respect women who are ambitious, focused and those who stay true to themselves. It's easy to lose sight of who you are in the day-to-day grind of work. But I genuinely respect those who are unapologetic and give others opportunities to be successful.

What would you recommend to a student just starting and dreaming of a successful career?
Be curious, ask questions, and don't be afraid to speak up. Be patient; know that your work will speak for you and help you develop and grow. Be ambitious. We are capable of more than we believe! Most importantly, enjoy your work.

What essential qualifications do you think will be needed ten years from now?
Adaptability to change! In this ever-evolving world around us, it's essential to be adaptable to change. It doesn't mean we have to keep changing, but we should be cognizant of the change and understand its impact on us as individuals and on our communities, organisations, and careers.

How would you describe your leadership style? What is your leadership motivation?
I value open dialogue with my team and the people I work with. I am very passionate about developing people and helping them reach their full potential. By the time I end my career, I hope I will be remembered as an authentic leader, capable of building long-lasting relationships and someone who has been able to influence people's lives and careers positively.

If there is a lot of work and you are under stress, how do you compensate?
Reading has always been a hobby of mine. Immersing myself in something completely

unrelated to work helps me reset, giving me a fresh perspective on work challenges and issues. Other ways are to call a friend, catch up or spend time with my family; movie night is a favourite!

Do you do anything to keep you fit physically or mentally, and how often?
More mental than physical. While I try to exercise in my life, I can't say I have been consistent. Mentally, I spend each day reflecting on my day; I spend ten minutes just thinking it through and planning the next day, doing things differently or better if needed.

What does it take to be a successful woman these days? What are the three top things successful business people should personalise?
I believe success factors are usually the same (for men and women) in the sense that you need to be fair, focused, determined, able to deliver and adapt to changing business environments. There is the added social factor for women, whether it is supporting your family, being a good partner, or raising children. Women generally feel more pressured to be good at all of it. I think everybody needs to personalise their priorities and choices. I never apologise for being a wife and mother, where sometimes my personal life may need more attention than work or vice versa. It's important to be true to yourself and establish your balance.

Is there a quote you favour that suits you? Or an important book you read that influenced you?
I always come back to Maya Angelou's Poem "Still I rise" and a quote I once read that stuck "I shall allow no man to belittle my soul by making me hate him", by Booker T- Washington.

What are your most important goals? Is there a difference for you between life goals and career goals?
Our personal and professional lives are so intertwined that it's not always easy to distinguish. For me, it's the feeling behind the goals that matter. I want to be happy! That happiness comes from achieving certain milestones and successes in my personal and professional life. To name some plans: always have a good relationship with my children, continue to have a supportive relationship with my husband and enjoy my work still as I grow further in my career and have a positive influence.

Malak Al Shaibani

What was the best piece of advice that you were given regarding your career and that you will never forget?
The best advice I received is to work hard and continuously learn, grow and support the organisation to deliver results. I was always guided to respect those I worked with, be loyal and trustworthy, and always be professional.

What has shaped you the most in your life? Is there any specific situation?
In life, we go through many experiences that shape us. During my childhood, my parents instilled in me the value of getting a good education. That was the number one priority in my family. I watched how my parents both worked to ensure that we attended private schools and travelled and learned about other cultures.

Who would you identify as your role model? Whom do you look up to and why?
I have many role models, men and women, that I look up to for different things, so it would not be fair to name one. I look up to my grandmother, a social worker who was sent to boarding school in Egypt at the age of 7 and became one of the leading women in Zanzibar. I had always admired her courage and resilience when times were hard, yet she remained strong, positive and hopeful for a better future. I admire women who have made their mark and have also done a lot to support other women at a regional level. To me, these are the true pioneers that I admire.

What would you recommend to a student just starting and dreaming of a successful career?
Know yourself and what makes you tick, and know what you want out of life and a career. A career is not a straight line. There will be curves and ups and downs, so build the strength and resilience you need and focus on your goals.

What essential qualifications do you think will be needed ten years from now?
I don't think it would be qualifications as much as attitudes, and I would think the most important is being curious and having a growth mindset that allows you to change and unlearn things to move on to build new skills in careers that we never thought could exist. I can see a future where certain professions will disappear in a digital world. However, this is already happening; new opportunities open up, so how do you reinvent yourself in a dynamic world?

External Relations Country General Manager / Shell Oman

What are the three things in life you are most proud of?
My family: I have two grown sons, a loving husband, and I am also a grandmother. My career achievements, and finally, I feel humbled and proud that I may have helped and touched others to be better and achieve success in their own way.

Do you do anything to keep you fit physically or mentally, and how often?
I work out five times a week, have a meal plan that I follow, and love reading and baking during my spare time. So, reading keeps me mentally challenged and more aware of what is going on around me. I read various books, from biographies to self-development and politics. In addition, I love cooking and especially baking. It allows me to release stress, and I enjoy getting the family together around a home-cooked meal.

What does it take to be a successful woman these days? What are the three top things successful business people should personalise?
I think we need to redefine what success means so that it is not a biased term viewed with a gender lens but neutral. Many women attain the C-suite with many sacrifices, or some still think that you need to give up everything else. However, for women, in my view, in the corporate world, you need to be visible, and you need to know what you want and be willing to go for it. Self-limiting behaviours shall be overcome by knowing yourself better and getting a good mentor or coach. Also, women need to look for an organisation that embraces diversity and allows them to grow.

Is there a quote you favour that suits you? Or an important book you read that influenced you?
I read a lot of books I enjoyed, and some even helped. My life philosophy is about the importance of self-awareness and self-acceptance. I think knowing oneself allows you to find true happiness. Focus on how you can grow into a better person. Instead of looking out, look inwards and then do what makes you happy. I think this is a journey that will have bumps and surprises, but it can help you grow.

What are your most important goals? Is there a difference for you between life goals and career goals?
Some of the goals between life and career merge. One may have an impact on another. I divide my goals into these areas:

- Family (taking care or spending more time and energy)
- Financial (financial independence and a comfortable retirement)
- Community (volunteer or support those in need financially)
- Career (achievements for the organisation and myself)
- Lifestyle (will change based on time and priorities)

How would you describe yourself in three words and what is your secret to success?
I am organised, reliable and creative. For me, my success has been based on hard work, always seeking to do better and taking a very professional approach to what I do.

Maliha Al Sulaimani

What was the best piece of advice that you were given regarding your career and that you will never forget?
My Finance Director told me this, and I found it very useful and live by it every day, "If you need help, ask for it. When you get tired, learn to rest, not quit."

What has shaped you the most in your life? Is there any specific situation?
The challenges I had to face while I was a student in the States. It was tough living abroad, especially being far from my parents and loved ones. But, on the bright side, I learned how to take responsibility and be self-dependent, which will benefit me so much in my future.

Who would you identify as your role model? Whom do you look up to and why?
My twin sister Majda is my role model simply because she has always encouraged and inspired me to be the person I am today. She gives me strength when I am weak and has been there for me through thick and thin.

What do you respect most in other successful women?
I respect how strong, confident and driven they are, yet humble and kind at the same time. They're not afraid to be themselves and stand for what they believe in and always take chances.

What would you recommend to a student just starting and dreaming of a successful career?
Find your passion and look for a way to make a living out of it. Do what you love. We spend most of our lives and days at our jobs, so I would highly recommend doing something that makes you happy.

If the entire world listened to you for five minutes, what would you say or what would you want to talk about?
I would encourage people to live for themselves and not the life other people want them to live. Always spread love and positivity. Life is truly short, and time on this planet is limited. Focus on what brings you joy and happiness. No one has ever become poor by giving.

How would you describe your leadership style? What is your leadership motivation?
I always believe in motivating and helping support my team members to be their best selves by offering guidance instead of giving commands, and I reward achievements. Integrity should be included along with honesty as they go hand in hand.

If there is a lot of work and you are under stress, how do you compensate?
This is very easy. I compensate with shopping, then online shopping and finally more shopping.

Head Of Business Development / VIS GLOBAL SOLUTIONS

"Don't wait for an opportunity. Create it."

What are the three things in life you are most proud of?
- How far I've come in my career.
- My good relationship with family, friends and colleagues.
- At the age of 24, I built my own house.

Do you do anything to keep you fit physically or mentally, and how often?
I love yoga and swimming, which I do regularly to help me reduce stress and anxiety.

Is there a quote you favour that suits you? Or an important book you read that influenced you?
Don't wait for an opportunity. Create it.

How would you describe yourself in three words?
- Ambitious
- Passionate
- Sociable

What is your favourite place in Oman, that you like to visit in order to relax and recharge your batteries?
I love going to Bandar Jissah beach whenever the weather is beautiful for people who love seclusion and are seeking tranquillity. Bandar Jissah beach is an ideal place to be, as the beach is surrounded by immense tranquillity.

Maria Sarfaraz Ahmed

What was the best piece of advice that you were given regarding your career and that you will never forget?
At times, people or situations will throw you into the fire, which may sometimes be the best way to learn. Conversely, the most challenging courses are sometimes the most rewarding.

What has shaped you the most in your life? Is there any specific situation?
When I wanted to give up, when people didn't believe in me, when I was told time and time again that this wasn't for me, I never gave up. Believing in myself truly shaped me and my future.

On the path to where you are now, what was the most determining step?
As an entrepreneur, any decision you know involves risk can be challenging to take. The toughest one is to ask yourself, should I try hard or let it go? Both are blessings, but both come with trial and error.

Who would you identify as your role model? Whom do you look up to and why?
It may not be a common one, but my 5-year-old daughter is my role model. Every day, she teaches me how easy it is to be happy. One should find happiness in the smallest of things. And how smiles and hugs and a little thank you can change your day.

What do you respect most in other successful women?
The inspirational mindset. It is not as common as it should be, but I think successful women look at other women as companions in success as opposed to competitors.

What would you recommend to a student just starting and dreaming of a successful career?
Make mistakes. Yes, make them. Make many, but don't repeat them. It's ok to fail, and it's ok to restart, even to start late. Your timeline is yours, and nobody else has the right to decide what works for you and what doesn't.

What essential qualifications do you think will be needed ten years from now?
It is a skill. Emotional intelligence is and will be the most critical skill that people will need to have. It will help people make better decisions, become more self-aware and empathetic.

Country HR Manager / BRF / GCCs first face yoga coach

If there is a lot of work and you are under stress, how do you compensate?
I take 5-minute breaks every 30 minutes to breathe consciously. If you can't take breaks, it will be hard to concentrate on the actual task. So taking short, frequent breaks is highly effective.

Do you do anything to keep you fit physically or mentally, and how often?
I take long walks, do meditation, and teach and do face yoga, which helps in breathing and relaxing.

What does it take to be a successful woman these days? What are the three top things successful business people should personalise?
In my experience, it is adaptability, persistence and hard work. But one of the most important things is to believe in oneself; no one else will do that for you.

What would you devote your time and energy to if you were to invest now, in your future best self?
Self-love. I think many people don't love themselves enough and then expect others to do so. It doesn't happen this way. Having healthy boundaries is very important, and success starts from within.

Is there a quote you favour that suits you? Or an important book you read that influenced you?
"Skills can be learnt, but attitude cannot." My favourite book is Ikigai.

If you had extra time of four hours a day, what would you do during that time?
I would spend more time with my family. Many times we get so engrossed with work and life goals we forget family is everything. Job is great but play and family time is everything.

What are your most important goals? Is there a difference for you between life goals and career goals?
Choose a career that becomes a life goal. One must have a passion for what one does. If you love what your profession offers you, it automatically becomes your life goal.

Did the Omani culture you grew up in have an impact on your career path?
Omani culture has taught me that being polite, kind and giving is extremely important. Omanis are highly empathic and sensitive people. It helps us understand others better, making us better equipped to deal with other people and see them as individuals. Oman empowers women as equal to men, and this is the most profound experience in this country.

What is your favourite place in Oman, that you like to visit in order to relax and recharge your batteries?
Oman is a beautiful country. I love the beaches, the mountains, and the landscape. If I want a break, I could book a hotel with a lovely beach, go off to the beautiful wadis, or book a night in the beautiful Jabal Akhdar since I have a thing for mountains. That's where most of my tranquillity lies.

Mariya Al Hashar

Did the Omani culture you grew up in have an impact on your career path?
I come from a family whose origins are from the eastern coast of Oman. In former times, the head of the family used to travel by sea for trade for a long time, during which the wife was responsible for the house, children and all duties. I can say that I grew up in an environment that guarantees women a space in decision-making and crisis management.

What is your favourite place in Oman you like to visit in order to relax and recharge your batteries?
Oman is a country with a charming character and a calm atmosphere. Even the capital, Muscat, allows you to recharge and rebalance. Pandemic allowed me to discover beautiful new areas and hotels in Oman. I like the great city of Sur and its old souks; despite its hustle and bustle, it is my constant and never-boring shrine.

If the entire world listened to you for five minutes, what would you say or what would you want to talk about?
We are all together in this world, despite the distances between us. We are all affected by the same thorny problems, such as global warming, wars, refugee issues and many other issues. We are one; let's devote our thinking and efforts and try to find solutions; life is too short; learn, explore, seek, find yourself a purpose and look for it for the rest of your life.

Meet up with new people who have different points of view than you. For sure, they will open up your mind for new experiences. We are created with a different mindset to learn and teach each other.

What do you respect most in other successful women?
I respect a woman for her self-respect and self-love. I appreciate that she does not change despite the changes around her. I am impressed by the woman, leader in work and iron in her kingdom. She loves herself and sees that her comfort is a priority on which those around her are happy. She has unlimited passion.

How would you describe your leadership style? What is your leadership motivation?
I like to adopt a democratic leadership style. I want to listen to the team around me, evaluate their opinion and discover their full strength. I always believe that each person has undiscovered powers; I like to help them be successful.

What are your most important goals? Is there a difference for you between life goals and career goals?
My goal is to reach stability at all levels. In addition, I aspire to learn new languages and travel worldwide to obtain a leadership position in which I exercise a positive impact that reflects on society and the world. I don't think we can separate the two. Work goals serve life, and life goals serve you at work.

Senior Business Development Executive /
Oman Convention & Exhibition Centre

What would you recommend to a student just starting and dreaming of a successful career?
Dreaming alone is not enough to get what you want. Striving is a condition for success. Every day is a new opportunity to learn, and learning is the key to success, so seek knowledge. Do not wait for opportunities, your waiting for opportunities is nothing more than a waste of time. Options come with effort and work. Please create your own success story, as its impact is substantial and will remain within you as long as you live.

What does it take to be a successful woman these days? What are the three top things successful business people should personalise?
The Renaissance in the Sultanate of Oman created great opportunities for women to be successful and pioneering in whatever field they find themselves in. For me, the most important pillars of success are to focus on self-development and learning. In addition, having self-confidence, maintaining composure in difficult times, and not quarreling with mistakes for a long time are also needful characteristics.

Do you live with a daily routine?
I am a person who loves routine, and I'm not too fond of change unless it is necessary. Work takes up a good portion of my day, and the other part I like to spend on cooking or sports. Nighttime is a sacred time for me. I want to prepare myself to read quietly before bed.

Which topics should humanity focus more on in the future?
Internationally, I think the refugee issue should be more focused on, just thinking that children suffer. Also, more attention should be on the subject of global warming and the environment.
Locally, we should focus on the tourism aspect in the Sultanate of Oman and the sustainability of its tourism components, showcasing this beautiful country as a tourist destination and investment zone right in the middle of the world.

What are the three things in life you are most proud of?
Proud to have been chosen as a representative of the Middle East region in the Future Leaders Council. I am pleased to be an ambitious working mother. The feeling of guilt that comes to me if I am late while my daughter is waiting for me proves that everything is fine. I am proud that I haven't let myself down to be who I am today with all my flaws, weaknesses, strengths, and glow.

Maryam Khalifa Al Amri

What was the best piece of advice that you were given regarding your career and that you will never forget?
You can be better than yourself. So when you face a challenge, always remember why you started in the beginning. Also, there is recent advice that I got, which is, "Every time you face a new and demanding challenge, it is because you are moving to the next level in your life."

What has shaped you the most in your life? Is there any specific situation?
Being the oldest daughter with five brothers shaped me. I had to prove to them that I could be better at everything. So I steadily became a better version of myself through everyday situations, even if the reason was not quite right from today's perspective. Besides, especially reading made me a different, improved person and opened my eyes to other things in our culture or education system. I was hungry to learn new things and try to understand the world. At that time, we didn't have the internet or many connections with foreign countries. So, through reading, I discovered other worlds.

Who would you identify as your role model? Whom do you look up to and why?
My father, a pilot and independent person, a reader, and an adventurer. Family care is still his priority; he is a hard worker and a good life planner. The second person of my life I met at university. He was like a coach and tried to answer my deep questions about life at that time. Now we are best friends, and he joined me as a cofounder in my social enterprise. The third person is my mother. She sacrificed a lot for us, and she still tries her best to keep teaching us in life.

What would you recommend to a student just starting and dreaming of a successful career?
Learn as much as you can from life. Experience everything and go out of your comfort zone. Don't reject any opportunity that will give you new perspectives and skills. Learn.

If the entire world listened to you for five minutes, what would you say or what would you want to talk about?
If we want this world to be a better place, we should start with self-awareness, heal ourselves from the inside, and reflect. Taking care of your soul is the most important thing you should focus on. Being stable and peaceful inside will make you strong and prepared for any storm in your life.

How would you describe your leadership style? What is your leadership motivation?
One of them is inspirational leadership, and the other primary type is coaching leadership. My motivation is my mission in my life, which is making leaders everywhere through motivation and coaching. I try to uplift and to give opportunities and an environment to lead, especially women. Seeing them flying after all this training motivates me and makes me proud.

Founder & CEO / Youth Vision

If there is a lot of work and you are under stress, how do you compensate?
I have a morning routine to be balanced. Before I start my day, I write a morning journal and put all my thoughts, feelings, fears, expectations etc., on paper to relive them first and focus on the day's tasks with a very high energy level.

What are the three things in life you are most proud of?
First, achieving my dream by having a social enterprise company (Youth Vision) that provides innovative social and sustainable solutions for youth issues. Second, my children bring light to my life and drive me to give more and never stop. They are my blessing in this life. Third, being a role model for Omani youth - inspiring and empowering them as much as possible.

Do you do anything to keep you fit physically or mentally, and how often?
Yes, I have two coaches for physical training and exercising (3 days per week at 6 am before I start my day) and a life coach who helps me understand myself, uplifts me and moves me to the next level in my life. Also, reading and writing my journals is helping me a lot to make me stable and balanced.

Which topics should humanity focus more on in the future?
Innovation and sustainability in all our lifestyles, mindsets, and work values. It is our future to innovate but at the same time think about sustainability in this world in all aspects.

What does it take to be a successful woman these days?
What are the three top things successful business people should personalise?
To have a very high level of self-awareness and a solid social support system or groups that motivate. Be confident and resilient in life. Stick with your passion, regardless if people have different opinions.

Is there a quote you favour that suits you? Or an important book you read that influenced you?
Yes, I have a quote. "All our issues in this world will be solved with love and peace".

If you had extra time of four hours a day, what would you do during that time?
Meditate and walking in nature as much as I can.

Moza Ibrahim Al Azri

What has shaped you the most in your life? Is there any specific situation?
When I was thirteen, my parents and I moved to Australia, where I completed high school as my mother took her Master's Degree. Living abroad at a pivotal age in developing my personality allowed me to mature quickly, adapt to experiences outside my comfort zone. In addition, witnessing my mother's hard work and determination for success has shaped my perception of the role and impact of the Omani woman in society.

Who would you identify as your role model? Whom do you look up to and why?
My role model and biggest influencer is my mother. She built a successful career with around 200 employees. She was highly respected and very much loved. She was smart, in control, yet kind and deeply cared for by her teams. A true leader that both men and women were proud to follow. Often, I hear people say women are 'soft' or 'moody'; however, I genuinely believe we have a strong advantage when it comes to leadership. Women are highly intellectual, have a deep sense of self, have high interpersonal skills and know the right balance in leading from the mind and heart.

On the path to where you are now, what was the most determining step?
It all starts with self-awareness. When you know yourself, you are empowered, and when you accept yourself, you are invincible. Personally, my most decisive step was identifying my 'ideal self' and setting an intention to adopt daily habits that enable me to become her. What time does she wake up? What is her morning routine? What does she eat? How does she end her day? What time does she sleep? I encourage you to ask yourself these questions. To begin on a new row please. With the same resources at your disposal within a 24-hour day, who is your ideal self?

Is there a quote you favour that suits you? Or an important book you read that influenced you?
"Strive not to be a success, but rather to be of value" by Albert Einstein is a quote that reflects my outlook on life. A book that helped me navigate my way to leading a new team and manage to transition is "The First 90 days" by Michael D. Watkins.

Business Development Director, Acting / Oman Sail

What would you recommend to a student just starting and dreaming of a successful career?
Adopt a positive and professional attitude. It's essential to be consistent, think innovatively, be a team player, stay focused and always be proactive. Your qualifications will help get your foot in the door; however, your attitude will determine your success. Don't have the 'it's not my job' mentality and step up whenever an opportunity presents itself.

What essential qualifications do you think will be needed ten years from now?
I believe digital literacy will play, and it's crucial to be able to adapt to innovative solutions. When it comes to skill sets required, I think team spirit, leadership and communication skills will never go out of style.

What does it take to be a successful woman these days? What are the three top things successful business people should personalise?
It takes hard work, consistency and finding ways to be visible to get recognised. My top three advice to entrepreneurs is finding a unique selling point that sets you apart in the market, investing in targeted marketing, and ensuring excellent customer service.

If there is a lot of work and you are under stress, how do you compensate?
Oman is a country that has always empowered women and will continue to pave the way for female leaders in all industries. I believe to be successful, you need to work hard, be consistent, networking and being visible in order to be recognized.

When the pressure is exceptionally high, I tend to look for ways to disconnect and compensate for my efforts. That could be by taking a trip to spend quality time with family, painting, or just watching a good movie.

How would you describe yourself in three words? Do you live with a daily routine, and what is your secret to success?
Yes. Being a morning person, I like to start my days early by being active before heading to the office. In the evenings, I spend time with my family, and I usually do some light reading. Thus, my days are pretty structured as I think I can do more when I am organised. My support system, my positive attitude, team spirit, hard work and proactive nature have led me to where I am today.

What are the three things in life you are most proud of?
I am grateful and very proud of my family. Being career-driven, I'm thankful for a robust support system to motivate and a husband that matches my work ethic. I am also immensely proud of my parents' journey and the life they've built. They are my role models and a vital source of motivation. Finally, I'm proud of my country and to be an Omani woman under the leadership of His Majesty Sultan Haitham bin Tariq Al Said. I feel inspired every day to contribute towards Oman Vision 2040.

Moza S. Al Wardi

What was the best piece of advice that you were given regarding your career and that you will never forget?
Work with passion!

What has shaped you the most in your life? Is there any specific situation?
Many situations in my life have shaped and made me who I am today. When I was a child, we always spent our summer holidays visiting our family in the village. Behind the house, there is a historical grand mosque, which is called Al-Wardi grand mosque. Also, along there are old houses that were used in the past. The mud-brick mosque is not used as there are only walls and pillar remains. I enjoy going to these places where I can imagine life In the past. That influenced what I decided to study and work today. I always imagined how I could restore this mosque and reuse it. At that moment, I started researching Heritage and Cultural Management and began to look for Universities, and I found it available in Australia. That's where I studied an alternative, and I have enjoyed working in the field till this moment.

On the path to where you are now, what was the most determining step?
The most decisive step was to stay working with my team. Although, even when I got many job opportunities, I decided to be loyal to the National Museum project and stayed there.

What do you respect most in other successful women?
I respect that they are working with passion and enjoying what they are doing.

What would you recommend to a student just starting and dreaming of a successful career?
The students shall find out what they love to do. Find a direction and be successful and unique. But most importantly, love what you are doing!

What essential qualifications do you think will be needed ten years from now?
The following areas will be necessary for people and nations: health care, heritage and culture, technology, sustainability in agriculture and economic sustainability.

How would you describe your leadership style? What is your leadership motivation?
Being a good leader, you shall have the ability to be innovative, self-confident and you should also have the ability to motivate and inspire people. My leadership motivation has always been my passion and my sense of responsibility.

If there is a lot of work and you are under stress, how do you compensate?
If I am at work, I take a five minutes break and clear my mind with a cup of excellent coffee. Otherwise, after a week of stress, I take one day off to enjoy it with my family outside the city to refresh my mind.

Director of Collections Dep. / National Museum in Muscat

What are the three things in life you are most proud of?
I am proud of my achievements in the National Museum. I learned so much about my nation's history, which makes me proud, as well as my family.

Do you do anything to keep you fit physically or mentally, and how often?
Physically, I walk at the beach. I feel that the sea takes away all my stress.
Mentally, camping with my family (during the winter) and spending our weekend at our cottage in the countryside.

What would you devote your time and energy to if you were to invest now, in your future best self?
I would go back to university - where I would finish my Master's and PhD degrees. Also, to be able to contribute to the development projects on preserving the Omani heritage and culture.

If you had extra time of four hours a day, what would you do during that time?
I am at work in the morning, and after work, I spend time with my family. But if I had extra time during the day, I would spend it with my family or go shopping and get a cup of coffee.

What are your most important goals? Is there a difference for you between life goals and career goals?
I believe there is a link between life goals and career goals. My most important goal is to be healthy and be able to care for my family. Also, I like to learn from our life and career and share that knowledge with others. Finally, I love to be creative, unique and happy.

How would you describe yourself in three words? Do you live with a daily routine, and what is your secret to success?
At my work, there are constant challenges, so I don't live in a daily routine. However, I am ambitious and creative and a helpful person. My confidence, honesty and passion are factors for my success. In addition, it makes me happy if I can help and share my knowledge with others.

What is your favourite place in Oman, that you like to visit in order to relax and recharge your batteries?
I love camping outside the city on the beach.

Muntaha Al Zarafy

What was the best piece of advice that you were given regarding your career and that you will never forget?
"There are always three sides to every story." At the beginning of my career, I would always rush to a conclusion. However, it helped me navigate situations much better; once I understood that everyone has a different framework of thinking and reacting.

What has shaped you the most in your life? Is there any specific situation?
In one organisation, I had the complete technical skills to do my job correctly. However, I quickly learned that this is useless if I lack the emotional intelligence to communicate. Most people view the politics of an organisation as a negative aspect, but I saw it as an opportunity because it taught me that communication is vital. If a person cannot communicate efficiently and effectively with their peers, they will never get anything done. The skills I gained in understanding how to deal with different entities and personalities took me to the next level in my career.

Who would you identify as your role model? Whom do you look up to and why?
My parents. My mother managed to teach us the skills that we needed. She taught my sisters and me that we should always go after what we want because we were never less than anyone else- and she would always say an Arabic proverb, "A woman's weapon is her job".
As for my father, there are not enough words to explain his role in my life. The one thing I

will say is that he truly is the definition of a success story on his own. And throughout his career, he remained humble and kind, something I hope to achieve.

What would you recommend to a student just starting and dreaming of a successful career?
Don't worry about what others think; only you know what you are meant to do and what your path should be. You might take many journeys and make many mistakes along the way, but all these lessons are being placed in your approach to teach you something and get you to a point where you will shine!

What essential qualifications do you think will be needed ten years from now?
Digital skills, knowing how to optimise, create and analyse content for any business.

What are the three things in life you are most proud of?
My children, Omani Women 2010, and being part of the workforce that started Mazoon Dairy.

Do you do anything to keep you fit physically or mentally, and how often?
In the winter season, I try to find new locations for hiking in Oman, and in the summer, keeping up with my children is exercise already! However, I do try to go to the gym occasionally.

Which topics should humanity focus more on in the future?
Channelling 'Feminine Energy' in the workplace. I am not referring to women's empowerment; rather, I am talking about females utilising their feminine energy in leadership positions. There is a common belief that to be a successful leader, we must channel our masculine energy excessively (being assertive, logical, strong, goal-driven etc.). However, I genuinely believe what we lack is the feminine energy when trying to lead; this includes being maternal, caring, empathetic, creative, collaborative, warm and many other social attributes that would help employees achieve their best potential.

What does it take to be a successful woman these days? What are the three top things successful business people should personalise?
Have thick skin. Stand your ground. Be yourself.

What would you devote your time and energy to if you were to invest now, in your future best self?
Start my own business, and I wish I had the time to learn more languages or further develop the languages I currently know.

Did the Omani culture you grew up in have an impact on your career path?
Although I grew up in Austria, the Omani culture is a part of my identity. I am truly proud to be Omani. In the field of marketing, we personify brands to establish tonality. However, if I were to display Oman as a human being, it is a magnificent soul that stands tall and is not bothered by anyone else; it is humble, unique, and beautiful in its own right. This DNA runs in every Omani.

Nadhira Ahmed Alharthy

What has shaped you the most in your life? Is there any specific situation?
Not being able to pursue certain things while growing up because of fear of judgment held me back, but it also fostered a sense of adventure for me. I realized I loved experiencing new things, and I began to have a passion for exploring. In constantly pushing myself, I found there are many opportunities for learning and personal growth, which I hope to continue doing.

On the path to where you are now, what was the most determining step?
The most decisive step to getting to where I am now was keeping my goal of climbing Everest a secret. I prepped for it both physically and mentally months before I ever told anybody my intentions to protect my dream from the perceptions of others.

I knew that once I heard people's concerns or opinions out loud, it could stain my vision of what it would be like and possibly set me back. Keeping it to myself was the best thing I could've done because I wanted to prove to myself that I could do it, and I did.

What do you respect most in other successful women?
I respect the ambition and resilience that successful women often have. It's motivating to see other women win, mainly because it sets an excellent example for young girls to follow their dreams.

What essential qualifications do you think will be needed ten years from now?
Though education is important, I believe there are so many more qualifying elements to consider in any field. An athlete wouldn't necessarily need to have great grades in math, and an artist wouldn't necessarily need a college degree. Of course, those things help, but at the end of the day, it's your character, the way you carry yourself, and the extent of your determination that will get you to where you need to be.

Do you do anything to keep you fit physically or mentally, and how often?
I'm always trying to do different things physically, and my exercises range from swimming to hiking to resistance on a rotational basis. Mentally, I look forward to having stimulating conversations with people. Talking about people's ambitions and ideas is something I'm passionate about.

Which topics should humanity focus more on in the future?
I believe people must care for one another and show compassion. We must constantly remind each other that we're important and loved. Building people up plays a huge role in their contribution to a better society. I believe the younger generations are already showing a lot more support to each other in that sense, and I hope the stigmatization of mental health continues to cease.

Deputy Director General for Girls Guides / Ministry of Education of Oman
First Omani woman to summit Mt Everest '19 | First Arab women to summit Mt Ama Dablam' 21

What are your most important goals? Is there a difference between life and career goals for you?
Of course, there is a difference between personal and professional goals for me. Professionally, I hope to continue climbing up the ladder in my job at the Ministry of Education. I want to make a real and tangible difference for our youth. I also aspire to pursue a PhD in educational development at some point to understand how I can truly achieve those impacts. In addition, I always have fitness goals I try to reach so I can keep bettering myself. I also aspire to encourage more women to try mountain climbing and eventually start a professional Omani female climbers' team.

Did the Omani culture you grew up in have an impact on your career path?
Omani culture has had an impact on my career in more ways than one. For one, what I do isn't exactly common, but given its rarity, it gives me a platform to promote individuality and perseverance. It also allows me to have a reliable and supportive network. It influenced the way I dress. I haven't seen myself represented in sports growing up as a hijab woman, and I'm proud to be part of that representation for future generations today.

What is your favourite place in Oman, that you like to visit in order to relax and recharge your batteries?
Valleys. It's no surprise I love nature, and yes, the valleys are hard to get to at times, but they are so worth it. Once you reach them, it's such a stunning view, and unbelievable quiet and serenity. They take some searching, but they're worth the find, and it's always a valuable experience and memory.

Nahla Al Balushi

What was the best piece of advice that you were given regarding your career and that you will never forget?
The best advice was to work hard toward achieving my goals and developing my skills to keep up with the fast pace of technological advancements. In addition, I was encouraged to stay out of my comfort zone and continuously explore new opportunities.

What has shaped you the most in your life? Is there any specific situation?
When my father passed away, it was a tough time for my family. That led me to prioritize working on myself and expanding my knowledge to make him proud. He has always motivated me to focus on my studies, and he taught me so many valuable lessons, such as always keeping my values, that have made me the person I am today.

What do you respect most in other successful women?
I respect their dedication and determination to accomplish their goals and compete with their male partners. I perceive that we complement each other, and our efforts working together can lead to better results in our workplaces.

What would you recommend to a student just starting and dreaming of a successful career?
I highly advise students to start to develop their skills at a very early stage and try to discover their capabilities and potential. Then, they need to take any opportunity to enrich their learning experience and work toward finding what they can shine in. Sometimes, it is not the degree you earn but your passion that defines your career paths.

If the entire world listened to you for five minutes, what would you say or what would you want to talk about?
I would want to talk about climate change. I want to significantly increase awareness as only together can we save our planet from all the horrific damage we have done to it over the years.

Head of Information Security Department / Central Bank of Oman

What essential qualifications do you think will be needed ten years from now?
In the fourth industrial revolution era, the qualifications needed will change dramatically, and some might disappear completely. However, some capabilities that I think will be in demand are technology-related skills, problem-solving, innovation and creativity.

How would you describe your leadership style? What is your leadership motivation?
My leadership style concentrates on understanding the team and ensuring that it's a healthy environment where all opinions are considered. Also, I try my best to ensure that each person's capabilities are utilized productively.

Finally, my leadership motivation is to reach organizational goals without compromising quality. This is always best achieved by working as a team and involving all the members in the thinking process.

What are the three things in life you are most proud of?
I am proud of myself for balancing between raising 5 kids, my job, and earning my doctorate. My kids are always my number one priority. They are wonderful children, and they all work so hard in school. This is definitely my biggest achievement.

I hold much responsibility at work, and I am proud to say that I have won "Women Cyber Security Executive" in 2020. Lastly, I am proud that I am working to earn my doctorate and expand my knowledge.

Do you do anything to keep you fit physically or mentally, and how often?
I try my best to run on the treadmill every day, and I occasionally enjoy going on hikes and exploring new places. In addition to that, I read as many books as I can to keep myself mentally fit.

What does it take to be a successful woman these days? What are the three top things successful business people should personalise?
It takes dedication, strength, and consistency. A successful woman is a strong woman; breaking societal standards and working extra hard to prove yourself is not easy. However, anyone who wants to succeed needs to work hard to attain their position.

What is your favourite place in Oman, that you like to visit in order to relax and recharge your batteries?
My favourite place to go to is Jabal Shams. I went on a 10-hour hike, which was honestly so exhausting, but worth every second. The place is so tranquil and picturesque. Especially during the sunset, the sky looks so beautiful, and it feels like you want to sit there and look at the sky all day.

Najah Al Rashdi

What was the best piece of advice that you were given regarding your career and that you will never forget?
Keep Learning and never stop dreaming.

What has shaped you the most in your life? Is there any specific situation?
Good and bad have shaped me, blessings and pain; what I can recall is being challenged several times as a woman on several occasions to lead or solve issues. Not forgetting the number of times I had to stand up and fight for something I believed to be right, and the moment I won and succeeded, I would be so proud, proud in tears for having to put that much effort! And here I am now with a unique blend of softness and toughness all in one soul.

Who would you identify as your role model? Whom do you look up to and why?
Both my parents. Both were so determined, worked very hard, were humble, worked with joy, and loved their country.

What do you respect most in other successful women?
Persistence and the strength you see in them when everyone else thinks they have fallen. Successful women will get up and go back to the front line and do what is right.

What would you recommend to a student just starting and dreaming of a successful career?
Have a clear vision, plan right, revisit your inner self needs regularly, fine-tune your plans accordingly, focus on what you are doing, and consult the right person/s.

If the entire world listened to you for five minutes, what would you say or what would you want to talk about?
I would talk about morality, about the values that we sincerely carry in our hearts. The duty we have towards people around us, to inspire and spread good deeds. I would explain that the largest bank accounts and highest professional qualifications will never outweigh the principles of right and wrong! You can never be successful if you do not have the quality it takes to earn the title.

What essential qualifications do you think will be needed ten years from now?
Those that relate to the 4th and the coming 5th industrial revolution technologies. Any qualification will have to be attached to the elements of artificial intelligence and the internet of things, the engineering of autonomous vehicles and machines, the printing of homes and buildings and bridges, etc. Aside from all those sophisticated qualifications, there will be an increased need for counsellors and coaches.

How would you describe your leadership style? What is your leadership motivation?
Being part of a team, I make the decisions but pull up my sleeves and work hand in hand;

Director-General of Innovation Center /
Ministry of Higher Education, Research & Innovation

I involve them from day 1; we brainstorm, share thoughts as each one of us has learnt lessons from previous experiences, and some would have out of the box ideas that would fit very well. I spend time to be with them and listen to each one of them individually. The two most important factors for my success as a leader are communication and trust. Those are must-have ingredients in all my projects. Finally, my style gives each member a sense of ownership, which creates the magic in what we do.

If there is a lot of work and you are under stress, how do you compensate?
I put everything on paper, prioritise, delegate, if possible, plan for each task; once the plans with time-frames are clear, the stress will go down. I always start with breathing techniques and create a relaxed environment to analyse and then develop the proper plans.

What are the three things in life you are most proud of?
The person I have become, the personalities and qualities of my children, and the good impression I left and the beautiful relationships and connections I currently have with so many that I am so grateful for.

Which topics should humanity focus more on in the future?
Healthy lifestyle (enforcement, not just advice and social media talks), communication (all types at all levels), ethics, blending again with the natural environment.

What would you devote your time and energy to if you were to invest now, in your future best self?
I would maintain my physical and mental fitness, I would prepare everything to have a worry-free, stress-free, independent and peaceful retirement life. I enjoy my loving relationships, sustainable resources and personal interests.

Did the Omani culture you grew up in have an impact on your career path?
As Omanis, we are known to be very kind and caring; we help and support each other. And I have carried and implemented that throughout my journey.

What is your favourite place in Oman, that you like to visit in order to relax and recharge your batteries?
We are fortunate and blessed with a coast-line of beautiful sandy beaches, and I am so attached to the tranquil and unique beach sides we have and the magical sounds of the waves. To me, there is no better place to relax and recharge.

Najla Al Mayahi

What was the best piece of advice that you were given regarding your career and that you will never forget?
My mother's advice was to be patient. It benefits me in my career as well as in life. By nature, I wasn't so patient as I used to take actions very fast without thinking. I learned in my first job as a cabin crew to be patient. I learned to be less reactive and always have a positive attitude to avoid making wrong decisions.

What has shaped you the most in your life? Is there any specific situation?
In life, there are always ups and downs. It's how you react that shapes you. I have been to so many situations that I believe made me more robust, and I learned a lot from them, such as the sudden death of my father and the sudden sickness of my mother. The movement from a different industry sector in which I had zero knowledge (Aviation to Telecom) challenged me. Looking for stability and pursuing my dream to continue studying was my priority. Hence, it was essential to take that step, which turned out to be the best decision.

Who would you identify as your role model? Whom do you look up to and why?
My role model, I would proudly say, is my mother, a strong woman who raised six kids alone after her husband passed away when she was just 29 years old.

What do you respect most in other successful women?
Their determination, persistence, patience and following their dreams. Moreover, I respect inspirational, successful women who leave their fingerprints.

What would you recommend to a student just starting and dreaming of a successful career?
Keep on dreaming; never give up on your dreams, even if it would take time to achieve them. Sometimes life would take you on different paths; focus and stick to your goals. Focus and plan it right, and you will reach the destination that you wish.

If the entire world listened to you for five minutes, what would you say or what would you want to talk about?
Be kind, love, forgive and respect yourself and others. Show compassion, especially now with the pandemic globally. We all need to work together to give back to the community in any way we can (donation, volunteering, smile, inspire). Have a purpose in your life towards humanity.

What essential qualifications do you think will be needed ten years from now?
We are in the digitalisation era, so I think it would be digital technologies and artificial intelligence. But, nevertheless, social intelligence will be necessary.

If there is a lot of work and you are under stress, how do you compensate?
I always believe we can manage stress, and it's all in our head; once you are overloaded with

Senior Manager - Research and Market Intelligence / Ooredoo Oman

work, take a break. Even for 5 minutes, do something you love (drink coffee, listen to one of the motivational speakers, or just breath).

What are the three things in life you are most proud of?
- Raising my four kids.
- Certification (MBA).
- My relationship with my family and friends.
- Opening a business (event planning) to bring a smile to our customers.

What does it take to be a successful woman these days?
Women these days need to be risk-takers, ready to delve into the future with no apparent hope but constant certainty in the success of the idea they are working on with passion and motivation.

What would you devote your time and energy to if you were to invest now, in your future best self?
Investing in yourself is essential, as you will see the benefits in the future. Arm yourself with knowledge, read, learn, attend different pieces of training, focus on changing your weaknesses into strengths.

If you had extra time of four hours a day, what would you do during that time?
I would take the chance in mediation, as it is vital to be in touch with your inner space in this busy life.

What are your most important goals? Is there a difference for you between life goals and career goals?
Yes, there is a difference between life goals and career goals. First, my goal in life is to focus on my kids and teach them to be productive. The second is to have an impact on society, having many projects in mind. Finally, when it comes to career goals, I wouldn't say get promoted and have a higher position, but my motivation is to have new challenges and spread knowledge.

What is your favourite place in Oman, that you like to visit in order to relax and recharge your batteries?
We are so lucky in Oman to have the autumn season in Khareef, Salalah, which brings peace and relaxation after summer. Hence, I would say Salalah is my favourite place.

Nashwa Al Rawahy

What was the best piece of advice that you were given regarding your career and that you will never forget?
To never stop learning. This resonates with me daily, and I practice it with an open mind. It is a humbling piece of advice that has helped build my career. In an ever-changing world, the quest for knowledge is key to staying relevant and excelling professionally.

What has shaped you the most in your life? Is there any specific situation?
There are so many people, situations and experiences that have helped shape me in my life. At the top of the list are my parents. Having such loving, nurturing, and supportive parents laid the solid foundation for me to build my life and shape me into the woman I am today. They exposed me to some of the best this world can offer, including travel, quality education, and new experiences. Today, my wonderful husband, two beautiful girls and caring son help to keep me grounded and remind me just how beautiful and pure this world can be.

What do you respect most in other successful women?
Practising balance between work and life continues to inspire me. Prioritizing themselves as well as the demands of a successful career or demanding household is paramount. I have a deep respect for women who are as accountable to their own well-being as they are for their success at work. Being blessed to be a parent myself, I can fully appreciate what my mother accomplished and juggled between her successful career and creating a nurturing home, all with grace, humility, and poise. I feel blessed to have her as a role model and continue to strive to achieve a semblance of what she had embodied, carrying it forever in my heart.

What would you recommend to a student just starting and dreaming of a successful career?
Dream big, but keep your feet on the ground and focus sharply. Think about how you want to define and measure your success. You will be your biggest cheerleader, your own brand ambassador, and the key to your own future. Hold yourself accountable to avoid disappointment. Being at the right place at the right time is a real phenomenon, and if you are lucky enough to be in that position, take advantage of it and use it as a springboard for your career.

Director / HMR Consultants

If not, don't be deterred. Use every failure as an experience, learn from it, pick up the pieces, and move on. It won't be easy, but it will be worth the journey. Be flexible, quick on your feet, and adaptable to new situations. Stay open to new experiences, and never stop learning. Be humble. There is no task above or below you. Stay true to your values and let your ethics guide you. Maintaining your integrity and clear conscience is what counts. Be patient with yourself and trust your gut; it somehow tells you where you need to be before your mind can connect the dots.

What essential qualifications do you think will be needed ten years from now?
The World Economic Forum reports that 75 million jobs could be displaced due to the adoption of new technologies and structural changes in the labour market in the next 10 years. The pandemic and subsequent global recession have impacted everyone with the combined health, social and economic shocks. To forecast 10 years from now, the most important qualifications will probably be a combination of critical thinking, analysis and problem-solving skills as well as soft skills that cannot be automated, such as inclusive management, emotional intelligence, and basic social skills. The jobs that would stay in demand are health professionals, STEM (science, technology, engineering, and math) specialists, and innovators. There will also be jobs that don't even exist today in broader fields of climate change and AI psychology.

If there is a lot of work and you are under stress, how do you compensate?
I take a big step back and carve out time to be removed entirely from the source of stress. I go for a walk, exercise, play with my kids, go for a nice dinner with my husband, or just go for a coffee alone. It helps clear my mind and keep things in perspective, allowing me to organize my thoughts and address the situation with renewed energy, focus, and clarity.

Do you do anything to keep you fit physically or mentally, and how often?
Physical exercise is a necessary outlet for me. I love the endorphin rush after completing an intense workout. I exercise 3 times a week and stay active week-long by doing activities with my girls. This improves my productivity, proficiency, and positivity. Keeping fit is a lifestyle and helps keep my momentum going.

Is there a quote you favour that suits you? Or an important book you read that influenced you?
"Stay hungry. Stay foolish", by Steve Jobs. This reminds me of keeping my innermost spark and passion alive. Some of the greatest joys in life come from living outside of our comfort zones. Living boldly and with intent, pushing boundaries, and taking calculated risks is when beautiful things happen. Having the courage to follow my intuition and believing in myself helps fulfil my purpose.

If you had extra time of four hours a day, what would you do during that time?
Spend more quality time with my loved ones and save some moments for myself to decompress, spiritually connect and reflect. Time is the most precious gift you can give, as you never get it back. As the saying goes, happiness is not a destination and cannot be consumed. It is the experience of living every moment with love, grace, and gratitude.

Nasima Al Balushi

What was the best piece of advice that you were given regarding your career and that you will never forget?
When I started my first post after graduation, my supervisor advised me: "Nasima, you are going to be part of my team, and you will be dealing with financial aspects in the organisation; your career and growth will depend on how responsible and trustful person you are, so put these two advises in your mind in working with us." I considered this advice in all the responsibilities and positions that I have held. It helped me to grow and gain trust.

What has shaped you the most in your life? Is there any specific situation?
By being responsible for export development in my previous organisation, I travelled a lot to organise various events in international markets. In addition, I had to deal with people of different nationalities and backgrounds. These experiences shaped my personality, so I became confident, could take faster decisions and applied international affairs.

On the path to where you are now, what was the most determining step?
The most decisive step was to change my career in finance affairs towards a promotion and marketing career path. It required much effort to support exporting companies, guiding them towards internationalisation and dealing with international markets. There were many challenges at the beginning.

What do you respect most in other successful women?
I respect other successful women's self-confidence and the ability to make bold decisions without fear. I also appreciate the caring aspect that they have towards their employees. However, they also need to know how to have a work-life balance.

What would you recommend to a student just starting and dreaming of a successful career?
I want to advise them to be good listeners and learners initially, trying not to jump very fast in their career ladder, take gradual growth with continuous development in knowledge. Try to gain more skills to be able to adapt to the high-speed changing environment. Love what you do, do your job with passion, and be open to new ideas. Add value to any position you hold and put your country's prosperity as objective as you grow.

How would you describe your leadership style? What is your leadership motivation?
My leadership style is Laissez-faire or delegative leadership. This style allows me to delegate responsibility and decision making to my team members. I also think this leadership style encourages innovation by empowering self-motivated employees to engage with their passion. It also helps experienced employees to take advantage of their competence and experience. Finally, it creates a positive work environment.

Director General of Investment Promotion /
Ministry of Commerce, Industry & Investment Promotion

What are the three things in life you are most proud of?
I am proud to graduate from Sultan Qaboos University, where I studied finance and economics. I am proud of having a very supportive family who supported me during my study and career. I am proud of being able to help Omani companies get international exposure by assisting them to participate internationally and giving them the advice to penetrate different markets.

Is there a quote you favour that suits you? Or an important book you read that influenced you?
I like to read Robin Sharma. He is one of the top leadership experts worldwide. "The Monk Who Sold his Ferrari." This book is built on seven virtues of alignment and applying these to our lives. The seven virtues are mastering your mind, following your purpose, practising Kaizen, the power of discipline, respecting your time, selflessly serving others and embracing the present.

How would you describe yourself and what is your secret to success?
I describe my personality as being disciplined, resilient, and adaptable to different circumstances and being patient and result-oriented when it comes to achieving the KPIs. I also delegate to individuals who report to me and value their thoughts, and welcome their ideas.

Did the Omani culture you grew up in have an impact on your career path?
I believe the culture that we live in has an impact on our career path. It positively affected me. I can work with my male and female colleagues in the same working environment, receiving the same incentives and opportunities available for both genders. Competition is based on achievement and success. Therefore, sharing values within the organisation contributed positively.

What is your favourite place in Oman, that you like to visit in order to relax and recharge your batteries?
My favourite place in Oman is the land of frankincense Dhofar; I like to visit Salalah during the Khareef season and throughout the year. It's culturally unique and retains its authenticity. You can enjoy the tropical fruit and juices. The beaches are natural with sparkling blue water without the effects of pollution or overuse.

Najya Al Hinai

What was the best piece of advice that you were given regarding your career and that you will never forget?
Early on in my career, I had a manager that spent about 70% of his time coaching his team. When I asked him why he did this, he said, "Your team is only as strong as its weakest link."

What has shaped you the most in your life? Is there any specific situation?
If I must narrow down what has shaped me the most, it is becoming a mother. I aspire to be a role model to my children, set an example as my mother did for me, exemplify the values I want to instil in them, and more importantly, I want them to be proud of what I can achieve. Therefore, I am more conscious of my decisions, the type of work I choose to do, my contributions to society, and the impact I make.

On the path to where you are now, what was the most determining step?
I have worked as a health and safety professional for over 13 years in various fields. Although each job brings about its challenges, as a safety professional, your decisions impact frontline workers' lives. One thing that hasn't changed throughout my career is to stand up for what I believe in and strive always to do what will deliver the best possible outcome for the frontline workers.

What do you respect most in other successful women?
I believe success is subjective. To me, success doesn't necessarily mean a high earning position and title. Instead, success is about your impact on the organisation, society, and people around you. Over the last few years, I have seen more and more women who are determined to challenge the status quo, fight stereotypes, and tackle societal pressure to achieve their goals. I have admiration and respect for women who stand up for their rights and support each other to succeed and make a change.

How would you describe your leadership style? What is your leadership motivation?
A leadership style depends on the situation you are in. Of course, no one is right or wrong.

Continuous Improvement Lead / Petroleum Development Oman

Nevertheless, I tend to lean more towards servant and transformational leadership.
Servant leaders share power, put the needs of others first, help individuals develop and optimise performance, and the leader is open to listening, learning, and receiving solutions from their team. In comparison, transformational leadership focuses on idealised influence, inspirational motivation, intellectual stimulation, and individual consideration.

If there is a lot of work and you are under stress, how do you compensate?
Stress is inevitable. However, there are ways to minimise stress by being open with your line manager, discussing your workload, and prioritising and de-prioritising projects to get things done.
You must also understand your skill sets; I am fortunate that I work well under pressure. However, I recognise that not everyone is the same, so I am conscious of my expectations when working with others. I also realise the importance of my physical and mental health and the need to take breaks. I value my health, and finding a balance between work and life is essential.

Is there a quote you favour that suits you? Or an important book you read that influenced you?
Facts before feelings. I like to look at things logically. Usually, when a problem occurs, I ask individuals to separate how they feel from the facts. Having the points allows for a more holistic approach to problem-solving. Another motto is that what you put out into the world will come back to you. I believe the world needs more kindness, empathy, and humanity. So I try to live by these values.

What are your most important goals? Is there a difference for you between life goals and career goals?
My life goals and career goals do differ, although I think they intertwine. My personal goals now are to have a balanced social life where I also take time for myself to learn new skills or take on a new hobby. My career goals are to evolve my growth mindset, undergo a master's in industrial and organisational psychology, and enhance my qualifications in organisational change management.

How would you describe yourself in three words and what is your secret to success?
The three words I would use to describe myself and make me successful are: logical, caring, and hard-working.

Did the Omani culture you grew up in have an impact on your career path?
I am grateful for the Omani culture as we are so open to growth and improvement thanks to the late Sultan Qaboos bin Said. Women are educated and also encouraged to pursue their careers.

What is your favourite place in Oman, that you like to visit in order to relax and recharge your batteries?
Oman has some of the most beautiful beaches globally. Something about the blue waters and the sound of the waves is therapeutic to me.

Noura Mohammed Abdullah Al Dhahouri

What was the best piece of advice that you were given regarding your career and that you will never forget?
The best advice for me is that whenever you face any challenges or feel that everything will be complicated, take a few days off and then you will find and think clearly about solutions and how to solve these issues. When a door closes, try the window.

What has shaped you the most in your life? Is there any specific situation?
What shaped my personality was how my parents raised and empowered me. My father, a simple fisherman, taught me how to be unique and respect my thoughts and supported me always to follow my dreams and accomplish them, just like my mother. Since I was a kid, the responsibilities they gave me to run the financial things in the house gave me the power and the tips to be a leader. At the university stage, I felt that I must create a business to support me financially, just not to ask my family every time, and that's why I had a small business in printing research for students.

On the path to where you are now, what was the most determining step?
The most decisive step was when I decided to chase my dreams no matter where to go. So I studied and worked, and then I moved to the UAE. Specifically in Abu-Dhabi, where I worked before I moved back again to my town in Dibba. I completed my master's degree there and then moved back to Muscat to work in the Quality Department and set up my first physical store (vogue lane boutique) beside my online business (taqaseem).

Who would you identify as your role model? Whom do you look up to and why?
Anyone that teaches me something good in life will be my role model. However, I love the way that Mthayel Al-Ali is running her life. She is such a creative and talented woman.

Head-section of Quality Department / Ministry of Interiors
Owner of Taqaseem | Owner of Vogue Lane

What do you respect most in other successful women?
I respect the power that they face in the community's thoughts, how they try to support each other, and how strong they are to represent themselves.

What would you recommend to a student just starting and dreaming of a successful career?
A successful career may not only connect to a government job; you can start your own business, you will face plenty of challenges. However, these challenges will make you stronger and gain you more knowledge.

If the entire world listened to you for five minutes, what would you say or what would you want to talk about?
Well, I can say, don't let anything stop you from accomplishing your aims and dreams. Life is not easy, and that is the beauty of life. But you choose your work and grow yourself.

If there is a lot of work and you are under stress, how do you compensate?
First, I will make a To-Do list and prioritise the work based on the importance and the deadline; then, I will listen to my favourite music with a cup of coffee and try to finish the job. If I face any issues, I will get a hand from my colleagues to assist me.

What are the three things in life you are most proud of?
• The way of my life.
• My strong personality.
• My ambitious goal to do better and to achieve more.

What are your most important goals? Is there a difference for you between life goals and career goals?
The most important goal that I wanted to achieve in my career is to get a higher position that represents myself and empowers me as a woman from Musandam. I wish to be an ambassadress and to be a good role model for young women so that they can be anything that they want by being true and hardworking.

What is your favourite place in Oman, that you like to visit in order to relax and recharge your batteries?
The best place for me to relax and to get more energy is the beach in any area. Whether in Musandam or Alsharqyya. I love winter because I can do many activities such as walking in the morning, hiking, visiting new places, trips to new destinations in Oman to explore the natural beauty of my country.

Nutaila Al Kharusi

What was the best piece of advice that you were given regarding your career and that you will never forget?
Picking the right job is a lot of pressure on someone. There isn't just one "right job". There are many good choices out there, but you must ensure the choice you've selected is right! Perseverance, commitment, and passion are essential ingredients to your career.

What has shaped you the most in your life? Is there any specific situation?
I think witnessing the strain and impact my family, and I had to endure while my eldest sister suffered from her mental illness was a life-changing event that paved my career. It was tough on us as a family, especially my parents, to see their daughter ailing and feeling helpless since, at the time, Oman did not have the proper mental health treatment facilities. While being a passive spectator to my family's hardships, I knew that mental health was my calling.

Who would you identify as your role model? Whom do you look up to and why?
My mother is my role model. She is the epitome of a woman with grit, perseverance, optimism, determination, and courage. I have learned many lessons of patience, sublimation, dedication, and never-say-die-attitude from such a pillar of light. My mom's grit has also taught me that it is possible to start from very little and achieve goals that may seem unreachable.

What do you respect most in other successful women?
I admire successful women who are not worried about what other people think of a woman striving for a career. I admire women who are trying to pursue their dreams and who live life on their terms. I also respect that these successful women are good at balancing their careers and family and taking time for themselves to create personal space to enjoy something unique to them!

What would you recommend to a student just starting and dreaming of a successful career?
I would let students know that they can be anything they set their heart to. I would also warn them that they will stumble and fall at times, and the journey will be a bit bumpy, but they should hold on tight and not give up! Instead, they should continue along the way; acquire the support system and tools they need to pursue their passion.

If the entire world listened to you for five minutes, what would you say or what would you want to talk about?
I would say pay special attention to your emotions and thoughts. Dedicate yourself daily to self-love. Relish in every moment and be present. Practice mindfulness and meditation. Focus your energy on what you can control. Look closely at your behaviours, as these are what you can control. Embrace all thoughts and emotions with compassion and acceptance and see them for what they are: nothing more or nothing less; they are merely words and feelings. Remember to love yourself, believe in your ability to change, and be the change you want in this world. It's ok to cry, but afterwards, pick yourself up and push forward towards the

Psychologist & Managing Director / Al Harub Medical Centre

prize. Align your behaviours with what you value. Sprinkle your values on your day. And remember, everything begins and ends with You. You are important.

What essential qualifications do you think will be needed ten years from now?
I think social and emotional skills are going to be necessary. Communication, solving problems, adapting, empathising, and tolerating stressful situations are essential skills. Moreover, critical thinking skills and technical IT skills are crucial as well!

If there is a lot of work and you are under stress, how do you compensate?
I am good at tuning in to my body signals. I pause and identify the thoughts and emotions that I am experiencing, and then I proceed with the appropriate behaviour. I think checking in with yourself from time to time will prevent one from burning out as you are in sync with your feelings and thoughts. For example, when my body signals to me that I am stressed, I pause and align myself with what I require at that moment, be it laying down, going for a walk in nature, spending time with my children, reaching out to friends, or even just reading a good book or watching a movie.

What are the three things in life you are most proud of?
My daughter Amara and son Aymen. The work I do as a therapist, guiding people - is gratifying and uplifting. My resilience: never giving up and being mentally flexible.

Do you do anything to keep you fit physically or mentally, and how often?
I exercise at least 3-4 times a week! After each workout, I do a mindfulness exercise, which helps me stay grounded, and by default, I become more relaxed! I also do a gratitude exercise every morning that lifts my spirits and sets my morning right. In addition, I journal three times a week, which I believe is a healthy channel to express my thoughts and feelings.

Which topics should humanity focus more on in the future?
Mental health is vital. I believe it is imperative to have courses in school for kids to learn how to look after their mental wellbeing and how to identify and navigate their feelings.

Rahma Al Hinai

What was the best piece of advice that you were given regarding your career and that you will never forget?
My mother's advice: "Education and work are your best friends in this life to be successful and robust, so you must be serious about your career," as she always said: "A woman can do anything."

What has shaped you the most in your life? Is there any specific situation?
In general, difficult situations and challenges recharged my life with a lot of patience, challenge, and courage to face life with strength and steadfastness.

What do you respect most in other successful women?
Strength, courage, and boldness in making important decisions. Self-reliance. Commitment to morals and values. Power of word and thought.

What would you recommend to a student just starting and dreaming of a successful career?
I advise the student first to strive hard and market themselves in professional platforms before graduating from college to have public relations that facilitate obtaining a job or training. Then, after employment, I advise them to work hard, trust and be patient to reach what they desire.

If the entire world listened to you for five minutes, what would you say or what would you want to talk about?
Sometimes you don't know the value of a moment until it becomes a memory, so focus on every moment in your life to do your best and leave a lasting memory. Go, travel, explore, live happily and smile.

Founder and Managing Director / brandin

If there is a lot of work and you are under stress, how do you compensate?
I stop working for a certain period and gather my energy by doing my favourite activities and sometimes doing quick exercises to relax and breathe.

What are the three things in life you are most proud of?
I am proud of my mother; she is an amazing woman and a fighter, and she was my best supporter.
I am also proud of my husband, as he is an exceptional husband who always supports me in developing myself and being successful in life. Finally, I pride myself on perseverance, being strong and never giving up.

Do you do anything to keep you fit physically or mentally, and how often?
Yes, I do sports and read books almost daily. What does it take to be a successful woman these days?

What are the three top things successful business people should personalise?
Her faith in herself, hard work, and correct marketing of professional and personal skills or business projects.

What would you devote your time and energy to if you were to invest now, in your future best self?
*   My company (Brandin), for graphic design and marketing.
*   Family life - raising my children.
*   Volunteer work.
*   Travelling and exploring the world.

Is there a quote you favour that suits you? Or an important book you read that influenced you?
"If you see everyone walking against you, do not hesitate to walk even if you are alone, for loneliness is better than living against yourself to please others", William Shakespeare.

If you had extra time of four hours a day, what would you do during that time?
I would do more sports, read more books, and watch movies.

How would you describe yourself what is your secret to success?
*   My power of thought and opinion
*   My love for learning and development
*   Challenge and patience

Did the Omani culture you grew up in have an impact on your career path?
Yes, the Omani culture in which I grew up taught me a commitment to values and principles - courage and strength - independence - the power of word and opinion.

Rawan AlMahrouqi

What was the best piece of advice that you were given regarding your career and that you will never forget?
If I don't do it myself, it will not happen. It's a reminder about taking charge of your life rather than waiting for other things to happen to change it for me.

What has shaped you the most in your life? Is there any specific situation?
My childhood is a big part of who I am today and my coming of age.

On the path to where you are now, what was the most determining step?
It is definitely to get up every morning and choose to go forward with my work. I always take active steps to reach my goals. That is both the most difficult and the most decisive step.

What would you recommend to a student just starting and dreaming of a successful career?
Experiment as much as you can, try as many different things as possible, and do something outside of your comfort zone. It's scary at first, but you will not regret it!

How would you describe your leadership style? What is your leadership motivation?
I would say my style is very relaxed but also very aware of my goals and aspirations. I like the work to be done in comfort, but it needs to be done at the end of the day.

If there is a lot of work and you are under stress, how do you compensate?
I allow myself to take breaks when I need to; I cannot function if I'm not there emotionally and mentally. So I need to take time off and come back when I am 100% ready.

Do you do anything to keep you fit physically or mentally, and how often?
I try to meditate every morning, or at least as much as I can. This is because meditation and mindfulness help me so much in staying afloat in my everyday life.

What does it take to be a successful woman these days? What are the three top things successful business people should personalise?
Successful people should always be open to new opportunities and always ready to support others.

Is there a quote you favour that suits you? Or an important book you read that influenced you?
'A New Earth' by Eckhart Tolle has been one of the most influential books that I like to go back to every once in a while.

Conceptual Artist / Founder of Makan Studios

What are your most important goals? Is there a difference for you between life goals and career goals?
Yes, I think there is a difference, but they are still connected somehow.

Did the Omani culture you grew up in have an impact on your career path?
Not on my career path because it's an unusual path to take in Oman, but it has impacted my career because most of my work is inspired by living in and being a part of the Omani culture.

What is your favourite place in Oman, that you like to visit in order to relax and recharge your batteries?
I have two go-to spots in Oman that make me feel better, the beach or the mountains.

Reem Alzadjali

What was the best piece of advice that you were given regarding your career and that you will never forget?
The best advice I got was from my father. He told me to always work with integrity and to do my best, and that will always make him proud, no matter what the outcome is.

On the path to where you are now, what was the most determining step?
The most powerful step was to open up my law firm and build up my reputation as a successful lawyer.

Who would you identify as your role model? Whom do you look up to and why?
My late father worked very hard and reached his goals at a young age. We are five girls and two boys, and he never treated us differently. I always admired him for his support of his family and everyone who would reach out to him for help. He supported the development of education and opened the first college of engineering in Oman. Any profits he got would go for students who could not afford to pay their college fees. He taught me that when you do good, you do it in silence and never think that you are better than others, for we are all equal.

What do you respect most in other successful women?
I respect that they have succeeded in multitasking! As we come from the middle east, it's a cultural thing where even if a woman works, she still takes the responsibilities of raising the kids and taking care of her home. So when you see a successful woman, you know that she worked very hard to get to where she is.

How would you describe your leadership style? What is your leadership motivation?
I always lead by example! I make sure that my team understands us as one family and that when one of us succeeds, it is a success for all of our team. I am very particular about every person who works with me. My leadership motivation is my kids, as I want them to be proud of me and see me in the same light as I saw and will always see my late father.

If there is a lot of work and you are under stress, how do you compensate?
Since the pandemic started, it has been difficult for many of us as we used to take holidays and short breaks now and then to travel and come back fresh. The best way for me is to sleep early and wake up the next day with positive vibes.

What are the three things in life you are most proud of?
I am proud of receiving an honour from Al Sayyida Al Jalila, wife of his Majesty Sultan Haithem, which was a feeling I will never forget; here I was being appreciated by my country for the work I do. I have also made my father so proud of me in the last days of his life. Secondly, I am proud of my law firm, which I established in a short period - that was my dream since I was little. Thirdly, publishing my book was an idea I had for many years. Still,

Founder / Reem Al Zadjali Lawyers & Legal Consultants

I did not have enough experience to write a general simplified book that included all the Omani laws related to women and finally published it in two languages.

Do you do anything to keep you fit physically or mentally, and how often?
I think it is essential to do at least one activity. For example, I have a private ballet class once a week at the weekend; it helps me destress and calm while it is a good exercise at the same time.

What does it take to be a successful woman these days? What are the three top things successful business people should personalise?
First, never let anyone put you down. Second, balance your work and family time. And third, take support from family members or friends. I think that successful business people should be transparent, communicate clearly and genuinely with clients.

What would you devote your time and energy to if you were to invest now, in your future best self?
For me, investing in my kids is my future.

What are your most important goals? Is there a difference for you between life goals and career goals?
The most important goal is to keep a good reputation, and this should be a life goal and a career goal; because reputation gives you success, especially as a lawyer.

Did the Omani culture you grew up in have an impact on your career path?
The Omani culture impacted me as I grew up genuinely helping others, which is part of our Omani culture. Hence, I always try to do pro bono work and free legal advice to those in need to give back to the community, which is part of our culture.

What is your favourite place in Oman, that you like to visit in order to relax and recharge your batteries?
One of my favourite places is Alila Hotel in Jebel Al Akhdar

Rehab Al Lawati

What was the best piece of advice that you were given regarding your career and that you will never forget?
If you are passionate about a particular subject and are eager to learn and grow in that space, then foresee the likely paths of career growth and establish for yourself a development framework based on those inputs, pursue relentlessly, and don't hold back.

What do you respect most in other successful women?
I intensely respect the camaraderie exhibited by successful women. There is no one better than us women who can empathise and understand our situation as we try to balance our duties and

aspirations towards family and work. Furthermore, I deeply respect women leaders who build a better environment and culture for women and men in their workplace, empowering them and believing in them.

What would you recommend to a student just starting and dreaming of a successful career?
Identify a mentor or a sponsor early on in your career. Ensure they know and understand your strengths and aspirations and engage in open and constructive two-way dialogue. Set short and long-term goals for yourself. Don't be shy about putting your hand up and communicate clearly.

How would you describe your leadership style? What is your leadership motivation?
As a leader, I see my EQ as a strong competence that I've developed and consider it an integral part of my leadership toolset. My empathy with my colleagues and subordinates pays off. As a result, the loyalty, productivity and effort people put in working with me is amplified. I can think of the following emotions as the most valuable for a leader: optimism and motivation. If I can foster an optimistic environment, our conscious and calculated optimism will convert challenges into opportunities. Small and large success and acknowledging them are part of the positive culture that creates a positive sustaining loop of motivation.

If there is a lot of work and you are under stress, how do you compensate?
Enjoying work is an essential first step to handling the stress associated with too much work. I ensure that I am in roles where I enjoy the work and new aspects as it evolves. I also confirm

Chief Operating Officer / Rakiza - Oman's Infrastructure Fund

that I am self-aware and recharge my energy pool. Some of the energy recharge mechanisms that work for me include spending time outdoors. Walking barefoot on the beach as a form of earthing is immensely calming. Observing, reflecting, and appreciating the blessings helps rebuild purpose and hence the energy to continue will resolve.

Do you do anything to keep you fit physically or mentally, and how often?
I exercise regularly, CrossFit at least three times a week, early in the morning. I endeavour to walk/jog for 30 minutes a day on the remaining weekdays, which I typically do close to sunset and is part of my earthing. Mentally, I start my day by reading relevant topics to my field and issues of personal interest. I enjoy listening to podcasts while driving. I ensure I have sufficient "me" time. I also incorporate enough family time to build on positive interactions that help all of us mentally and emotionally.

Which topics should humanity focus more on in the future?
Digital transformation. I believe any business or opportunity we take must consider the role of digital transformation. Climate change is a very time-sensitive topic that should be taken more seriously; it puts everyone's life at risk and cannot be disregarded.

What does it take to be a successful woman these days? What are the three top things successful business people should personalise?
I feel balance is essential to be a successful woman - the balance between your work and family. Setting up your boundaries and priorities is very important to enjoy what you are doing.
Three top things to personalise:

To build a culture of diversity and inclusion. The value-added, diverse perspectives, experience and thought process the diversity brings to the business cannot be overlooked. Intentional investing; be aware of your society and responsibility; and how your business affects your community.
Invest in your network.

Is there a quote you favour that suits you? Or an important book you read that influenced you?
"Sometimes challenges are thrown your way. That's your moment to shine and show what you are capable of. Maybe that's not the door you wanted to open but certainly opens other doors".
"Lean In", by Sheryl Sandberg. This book had a substantial positive impact on me during my career, and I enjoy listening to it. We, women, tend to undermine our strengths and capabilities compared to men. We need to put ourselves out there and take the opportunities, even if we didn't get all the skills required at a particular time.

How would you describe yourself in three words? What is your secret to success?
I would describe myself as multi-tasking yet highly organised and focused, ambitious and driven, setting short-term goals for myself as I enjoy new challenges and the learning that comes with them, and, finally, an open and honest person.

Riham Noor Al Zadjali

What was the best piece of advice that you were given regarding your career and that you will never forget?
My beloved late father said to me once that a career does not necessarily have to be something one likes to do; rather, it should be something one has to do. To my father, his career was a duty and a responsibility and not a privilege. He has a rich history of helping others, being the best in his field, doing what is right, looking at the whole picture, thinking of the future generations, and what benefits society. So his work and life had a meaningful, noble purpose. That is very motivational and enriching to me.

What has shaped you the most in your life? Is there any specific situation?
My beloved father is the one person who has shaped me the most, and quite naturally, leading by example leaves the most imprint on people. He despised hypocrisy. He never feared telling the truth. When he helped others, he made sure he did so in the most dignified way towards them. He never belittled children's opinions. He emphasised education and knowledge. At the height of his illness, he was still the kindest, compassionate, caring, and dignified person. I always think of my father in whatever I do.

On the path to where you are now, what was the most determining step?
To keep out of the public eye as I value my privacy. Therefore, I only accept interviews related to my work and think it could benefit others or improve my knowledge.

Who would you identify as your role model? Whom do you look up to and why?
My beloved late father. My father personified integrity, morality, honesty, honour, loyalty, sincerity, justice, strength, knowledge, hard work, love, kindness, understanding, compassion, dignity, pureness, goodness, and much more.

What do you respect most in other successful women?
I respect honesty, compassion, and professionalism.

Artist

What would you recommend to a student just starting and dreaming of a successful career?
To find out which field they lean towards the most, focus on being as professional as possible in that field of choice.

If there is a lot of work and you are under stress, how do you compensate?
I try to work on one project at a time. I organise a schedule where projects don't overlap. This lessens the stress and helps me give my best to each project. If projects do overlap for some reason, the thought that it is only temporary and that I can relax once it's over helps keep me motivated.

I also make sure my work and living spaces are always clean, decluttered, and organised. It helps me to focus on my task comfortably and efficiently, and I have no distractions.

If you had extra time of four hours a day, what would you do during that time?
I would finish more tasks on my to-do list or spend more quality time with family and read more.
What are your most important goals? Is there a difference for you between life goals and career goals?
I do not differentiate between life goals and career goals. My aim in both is to continue to work on myself and to leave a positive imprint.

Did the Omani culture you grew up in have an impact on your career path?
Growing up, seeing my father and his generation help build Oman during the renaissance period, where every citizen felt that they were part of building the country, instilled in me the love to work for the good of the whole and the future generation.

The social standards, beliefs, and traditions are why I volunteer for workshops and training programs and why I have started my initiative, and it also shapes many of my artworks.

What is your favourite place in Oman, that you like to visit in order to relax and recharge your batteries?
Any relaxing place with a view of the beach. We have many such places in Muscat. We are blessed with a beautiful coastline and sunny weather. The sun, the beach, and good company always recharge my batteries.

Another thing I do is attend artist gatherings or art movie nights at Stal gallery, which is next to my place and has become a second home to many artists here and to me. Lastly, my sister's place because nothing beats time spent with sisters to recharge.

Rumaitha Al Busaidi

What was the best piece of advice that you were given regarding your career and that you will never forget?
At the beginning of my career, a male colleague of mine sent me a quote that said: "Developing personal power means learning not to negotiate your self-worth for the sake of someone else or selling yourself short for a job". I appreciate that quote interaction every single day!

What do you respect most in other successful women?
Their resilience. Many women are shattering the glass ceilings as the first of their families to reach successful positions. Their capacity to pursue their goal, dream, objective, or wishes until the very end is something I admire. These women bend rather than break, move towards a goal beyond themselves, and keep sailing when others have already abandoned the boat.

What would you recommend to a student just starting and dreaming of a successful career?
Invest in yourself by learning the habits of the successful. Remember to be financially independent and not let anyone break your wings when you want to fly and soar to your goals and dreams. If anything, all you are is your ambitions and goals. Without them, the flavour of life will be lost.

If the entire world listened to you for five minutes, what would you say or what would you want to talk about?
I have been a TED Speaker. In my Ted Talk that has almost garnered a million views titled "women and girls, you are part of the climate solution", I highlighted the role of gender equality in combating climate change. Many may have had their eyebrows raised, but the connection is a lot more than you might think. Empowering women and girls worldwide is one of the most important ways to combat carbon pollution and is projected to reduce CO_2-equivalent gases by a total of 80 billion tons. My talk highlights how women are more likely to be impacted and displaced by climate catastrophes. I explain why access to education, employment, and family planning for all women and girls is the key to our climate future.

What essential qualifications do you think will be needed ten years from now?
To be a storyteller, communicator that frames the narrative to push people, business, and policies forward. This is one skill that no computer or program can ever replace, and it is growing to be more critical. According to the World Economic Forum, half of us will need to re-skill in a few years due to the "double-disruption" of COVID-19 and automation gains. As a result, we need innovation, analytic and critical thinking, active learning, and problem-solving skills more than ever before.

If there is a lot of work and you are under stress, how do you compensate?
I force myself to take a break and zoom out of the situation to reflect. Most of the time, this allows me to have a bird's-eye view of why things are overwhelming and re-adjust. We all tend to have triggers that push us into a stressful or anxious mindset, so mindfulness has helped

Founder / WomeX
Executive Board Member / Environment Society of Oman

explain why I feel the way I do. I most often take breaks in the form of hiking, long drives, or travelling, all while music soothes my ears.

What are the three things in life you are most proud of?
All personal achievements of mine that remind me how strong I can be against all odds:
Being the first female soccer analyst in the Arab World. Becoming the youngest Omani to reach the South Pole. Graduating from Harvard; my dream school.

Do you do anything to keep you fit physically or mentally, and how often?
I love walking while listening to music. I feel that this daily ritual of mine has helped me cope with it a lot. It has allowed my body to keep fit while my soul takes its rest.

What would you devote your time and energy to if you were to invest now, in your future best self?
I would invest in life-extending time, where my health takes number one priority. It might be the effect of living in the middle of a pandemic, but I don't want to experience a crushing wake-up call because I took my health for granted. I would also invest in multiple sources of income because no millionaire has a single source of income while they were working for their first million.
Finally, I would spend my time and energy in reflection and assessing how things are going. We need to do that more as a culture.

Is there a quote you favour that suits you? Or an important book you read that influenced you?
Eleanor Roosevelt's "The future belongs to those who believe in the beauty of their dreams" is one saying I truly live by and repeat for everyone to hear. I am a living example of it, and I want more and more of my fellow Arab women to follow suit and not give up because someone in society told them so.

Did the Omani culture you grew up in have an impact on your career path?
Most definitely, my entire personal and professional trajectory has resulted from how I interacted with my culture. Coming from a male-dominated society, many of my choices were frowned upon. Still, this fuelled my fire to excel at everything unconventional that I did, and I am who I am because of it!

What is your favourite place in Oman, that you like to visit in order to relax and recharge your batteries?
Bandar Khayran.

Safiya Al Bahlani

What was the best piece of advice that you were given regarding your career and that you will never forget?
"Don't always think in one direction; look at things from many angles, make the impossible possible."

What has shaped you the most in your life? Is there any specific situation?
The most important element that has shaped my life is the challenges I go through; it continuously teaches me something new and always motivates me to keep moving forward.

On the path to where you are now, what was the most determining step?
I believe in understanding my strengths and weaknesses instead of taking the usual or more accessible route.

Who would you identify as your role model? Whom do you look up to and why?
My mother is my role model; she never believed in the word "CAN'T". She believed in trying, trying, and trying until you have given it your all.

What do you respect most in other successful women?
I truly value and respect successful women who share the raw journey of becoming successful, not just giving the positive side of things.

What would you recommend to a student just starting and dreaming of a successful career?
For every dream you have, don't let it just be a dream in your mind; place it on paper or on your device or anywhere you can visually see it, create baby steps plans to get to that dream, believe you are living that dream already, feel it, think it, and make that dream a reality!

If the entire world listened to you for five minutes, what would you say or what would you want to talk about?
To truly get to where you want to go or be what you want, you need to first believe in yourself, don't wait around for others to give you a helping hand or to believe in you. Love yourself. By loving yourself, you accept everything about yourself, your strengths and weaknesses. Once you discover the love for yourself, you will start embracing it when challenges come your way. With every challenge you face, you grow another seed within you of a new skill or knowledge and leave a tiny print of achievement/victory. Don't forget to find gratitude and thank yourself for getting as far as you have on this journey.

Is there a quote you favour that suits you? Or an important book you read that influenced you?
Take the challenges as a tool to help you get closer to your goals.

Owner / Safiya Arts Gallery

What are your most important goals? Is there a difference for you between life goals and career goals?
The most important goals for me are being able to stand on my own feet and sharing and passing the knowledge I have learned through my journey to others that can benefit. I believe life goals and career goals are entwined, just branded differently.

What is your favourite place in Oman, that you like to visit in order to relax and recharge your batteries?
Oman is gorgeous. I don't say this because it is my country; I say this as a human being looking at the beauty of nature. I love taking my picnic chair and sitting on a mountaintop where I look at the openness and mother earth or the beautiful waters of Omani beaches. To me, being able to quench my thirst through nature's view recharges my batteries and always gives me a new angle to come back and work on whatever I do.

Sahara D. Hamayon

What was the best piece of advice that you were given regarding your career and that you will never forget?
Do not be afraid to take risks. Success usually lies out of your comfort zone. You'll uncover skills and more of yourself and your capabilities when you challenge yourself.

Who would you identify as your role model? Whom do you look up to and why?
My role model is Queen Rania of Jordan. She is an activist for the rights of women and children, promotes and supports entrepreneurship. Microfinance is an advocate of developments in education, healthcare and technology and is diligent in a mission to put an end to poverty and bridge cultural and educational divides. These are some of the many reasons why I look up to her and hopefully make a difference in this world, just like her one day.

What do you respect most in other successful women?
Strong work ethic, passion and drive they possess in their fields, the confidence, and their will for power. If the entire world listened to you for five minutes, what would you say or what would you want to talk about? Life is too short - we must live and let live.

We shouldn't be quick to judge and hate. Kindness is free, and you never know what one must be going through or have gone through. Be kind! No matter who or where they're from, be kind to one another! The world will be a better and safer place to live in.

If there is a lot of work and you are under stress, how do you compensate?
I like to delegate tasks to reduce workload and improve workplace productivity. If working solo, I want to give myself a deadline, and I try to stick to it as much as possible.

When there's a lot of work stress, I usually find solace in sports and fitness. An hour or two in physical sports helps me refocus and helps me, especially when I am stressed.

Do you do anything to keep you fit physically or mentally, and how often?
I train and practise Brazilian Jiu-Jitsu as well as weightlifting regularly, six times a week. Martial arts have boosted my self-confidence and taught me discipline in a healthier and better active lifestyle. It becomes an addiction, but you won't regret it in a good way once you see the fantastic turn that your life takes within a short period.

Which topics should humanity focus more on in the future?
'Human Rights', 'Putting an End to Racism' and 'Effect of Technology on our Future Generation'.

Brand & Operations Manager / Vivid Trading LLC

What does it take to be a successful woman these days? What are the three top things successful business people should personalise?
Commitment, self-discipline, courage and willpower.

What would you devote your time and energy to if you were to invest now, in your future best self?
In learning and improving my skills whilst exploring and travelling more.

Is there a quote you favour that suits you? Or an important book you read that influenced you?
My favourite line/motto in life is "Live and let live". The world is a better place if we all learn to accept one another for our differences, no matter who or where they come from. What makes us different is what makes us unique.

Did the Omani culture you grew up in have an impact on your career path?
I may not be Omani by blood, but for sure, Omani by heart and being born and raised here taught me a lot about the generous Omani hospitality, respect and importance of heritage and culture in every aspect of life, inclusive of career. Teamwork comes in naturally, and the drive to learn and grow is always there.

What is your favourite place in Oman, that you like to visit in order to relax and recharge your batteries?
The beach, wadis, or the beautiful scenic mountains like Jebel Akhdar and Jebel Shams.

Salha Al Ismaili

What was the best piece of advice that you were given regarding your career and that you will never forget?
After leaving medical studies due to financial constraints, a relative comforted me and told me that this could be an ending to a beautiful new beginning. He advised me to start in a role in the Human Resources field and asked me to acquire the knowledge and skills because he saw where I fit best. This advice was in 2008, and that's where my HR journey started.

On the path to where you are now, what was the most determining step?
Deciding not to remain complacent, I completed my higher studies irrespective of the situation, and I kept developing myself in terms of knowledge, skills, and abilities. And I will continue doing so.

Who would you identify as your role model? Whom do you look up to and why?
My mother. She never gave up, she never remained complacent, and she worked very hard to complete her studies at a time where it was not very easy, especially with having kids and responsibilities, and now completing to accomplish her retirement project goal and dream.

What do you respect most in other successful women?
I respect the passion for what they do; their persistence; the sacrifice they have to make to achieve their goals; their determination, confidence and, most of all, their leadership.
What would you recommend to a student just starting and dreaming of a successful career?
Take baby steps and always seek advice from an expert; have a mentor; self-develop irrespective of where you work or the situation, and focus on learning as much as possible. And never give up; keep going.

If the entire world listened to you for five minutes, what would you say or what would you want to talk about?
Never give up, never give up, never up. The hardest thing to learn in life is to lose, but it is a fact that we have to embrace; failure is part of the journey. On the other hand, good things come to those who wait. I have been through unpleasant times, but every situation was my stepping stone to reach a higher level of myself; every situation created a better version of me.

What essential qualifications do you think will be needed ten years from now?
I think the market now is focusing on professional certifications more than academic qualifications. Technology specialities will add value as the world moves towards digital transformation and COVID-19 forced us to adopt a new way of living.

How would you describe your leadership style? What is your leadership motivation?
I feel I am a natural-born leader. I read a lot about leadership, and my role model in leadership is the Virgin Group Founder and Chairman Richard Branson. What motivates me is my vision to learn more and inspire.

Career Development / Ministry of Health Oman

What are the three things in life you are most proud of?
I have a bucket list of things I am proud of, but here are my three most important things; my family, circle of friends who became my family, and home-based business, which I consider a hobby that I love.

Do you do anything to keep you fit physically or mentally, and how often?
My physical and mental health are very important to me. I practice yoga; it helps to keep fit and manage stress, in addition to the quality time spent with my family and kids.

What would you devote your time and energy to if you were to invest now, in your future best self?
I want to become an expert in Human Resources best practices and provide consultancy services in a few years. So I am dedicating time every day to equip myself with the knowledge and skills required to achieve that goal.

Is there a quote you favour that suits you? Or an important book you read that influenced you?
A quote that I love reading every day, and I have it on my desktop wallpaper "Don't be afraid to start again, this time you are not starting from scratch, you are starting from experience".

How would you describe yourself in three words? Do you live with a daily routine, and what is your secret to success?
Yes, I am living a daily routine. Highly organised, energetic, beautiful inside out. What makes me successful is my perseverance and insistence.

What is your favourite place in Oman, that you like to visit in order to relax and recharge your batteries?
Jebel Sifah, I have purposefully purchased an apartment there so I can escape the busy lifestyle, relax and unwind.

Salma Al Hashmi

What was the best piece of advice that you were given regarding your career and that you will never forget?
The one piece of advice I received, and have always valued, was, "Focus on doing your current job better than anybody has ever done it before."

What has shaped you the most in your life? Is there any specific situation?
Being thrown in at the deep end, which essentially means I unexpectedly had to take responsibility. The situation was challenging, but the experience I gained has served me well and encouraged me to be bolder.

Who would you identify as your role model? Whom do you look up to and why?
There are two people I like to acknowledge. First, I learned a great deal from Dr Amer Al Rawas, his leadership style, and team development. Even after he left his position in the company, his legacy lives on as it created a foundation that has allowed the team to continue to flourish. Second, I also admire Mr Mohammed Al Barwani. He was not handed anything in life on a silver platter and has worked very hard for everything he has achieved.

What do you respect most in other successful women?
Authenticity is essential. Truly showing who you are and taking a stand, and being known for having courage and confidence.

What would you recommend to a student just starting and dreaming of a successful career?
There are three things I would like to stress. First, take the time to learn, be patient and willing to learn from those around you. Second, it is essential to demonstrate commitment and dedication to your role, colleagues, and company. Lastly, and perhaps most importantly, choose a career in an industry that you are genuinely passionate about. Working life comes with many challenges, and passion sustains you, and it will help you keep thinking creatively.

If the entire world listened to you for five minutes, what would you say or what would you want to talk about?
Our common humanity. We must endeavour to find ways to preserve the humane aspect of life, which are all too easy to forget but without which we cannot indeed prosper.

Vice President Marketing / Al Mouj Muscat

What essential qualifications do you think will be needed ten years from now?
The emphasis will be less on qualifications and more on experiences and the incorporation of technology to further enhance the customer experience. It is crucial to adapt daily practices to modern innovations in order to maximise the positive impact an experience can resonate on a customer.

How would you describe your leadership style? What is your leadership motivation?
One of my favourite quotes that best describes my leadership and motivation style would be, "Great leaders don't blame the tools they are given. Great leaders work to sharpen them", by Simon Sinek. I believe in an inspirational leadership style that focuses on innovation, empowerment and influencing those around me.

What are the three things in life you are most proud of?
I have to say that I am proud of being a mother; I'm proud of my two sons, my husband, and how supportive my whole family has been. They are a blessing. I'm also proud of my team and the excellent organisation I work for, as I genuinely believe in our vision.

Finally, I am proud of my accomplishments and the life lessons that I have learnt. An important teachable moment is understanding that it is essential to face failure; taking responsibility teaches you a great deal, as people who understand and endure are those who achieve so much more.

Do you do anything to keep you fit physically or mentally, and how often?
I follow a fitness routine. I love running two to three times a week, and I combine that with sessions with my fitness instructor. I also do yoga. When it comes to mentally keeping fit, I meditate at least three to four times a week.

Is there a quote you favour that suits you? Or an important book you read that influenced you?
The book "Start with Why: How Great Leaders Inspire Everyone to Take Action" greatly influenced me. It points out how you shouldn't hire someone for their skills, but instead, you should look to hire them for their attitude. My favourite quote from the book is, "There are only two ways to influence human behaviour, you can manipulate it, or you can inspire it." I have found that this is the case, and it remains an essential insight.

How would you describe yourself in three words? Do you live with a daily routine, and what is your secret to success?
I follow Robin Sharma's 5 am club, including a 'power hour'. I wake up at 5 am five days a week and start my day with 20 minutes of fitness, followed by 20 minutes of self-development and 20 minutes of planning. This is not an easy process, and it takes time and commitment to get used to.
The three words I would use to describe myself are empathetic, reliable, and creative. If I had to sum up what I think makes me successful, it is perseverance and a willingness to keep learning.

(Dr.) Salma Mohamed Al Kindy

What was the best piece of advice that you were given regarding your career and that you will never forget?
During my undergraduate studies, I found myself at a crossroads whereby I contemplated switching majors from chemistry to economics because I was facing challenges with calculus, one of the crucial courses required for specialisation in chemistry. However, my academic advisor knew how passionate I was about chemistry and made me realise that I could overcome obstacles with determination and perseverance. She told me to learn that success comes through overcoming hurdles in life.

On the path to where you are now, what was the most determining step?
The most decisive step I took to pursue research and advance my career was when I accepted a Matsumae Fellowship (Foundation in Japan) to take up a six-month postdoctoral research fellowship in the Department of Bio-analytical Chemistry at Tokyo University. It was a challenging decision as it meant leaving my 10-month-old baby and children behind to be taken care of by my mother and my husband. This research led to scientific publications in reputable international journals, but it also enabled me to establish my research laboratory at SQU.

Who would you identify as your role model? Whom do you look up to and why?
I look up at my mother. I was fortunate that both my parents were working, and they provided me with the best example of balancing work and family. My curiosity about the natural world and fascination with education began with my mother as I watched her grade papers late into the night, and her passion opened my eyes to the possibilities of a career as a scientist. She was always available to support me, and she encouraged me to pursue my career and never give up on my goals. She inspired countless students, and I hope to do the same and keep her memory alive through my actions in the classroom.

What would you recommend to a student just starting and dreaming of a successful career?
We are living in COVID-19 times; remote teaching and learning are monumentally demanding and frustrating. Learners must be diligent, disciplined, and honest. They must keep abreast with the lectures and assigned course exercises during the learning process, bearing in mind that procrastination is the thief of time. Once you have identified the career of your dreams, the driving force in your studies should be the desire to achieve your goals. I would advise students to always aim at the highest and never settle for anything other than the best. Learn from failures.

If the entire world listened to you for five minutes, what would you say or what would you want to talk about?
There are two topical issues dear to my heart, namely gender equality and preservation of Oman's unique natural environment. First, the most promising, highly educated, and talented women should be recruited for top leadership positions. Second, the Sultanate of Oman has vast breath-taking coastlines, deserts, mountains, caves, and rivers, making it a geological

Professor of Analytical Chemistry / Sultan Qaboos University

paradise! Therefore, we need to prioritise an eco-friendly and green philosophy in science that helps conserve Omans' countryside.

How would you describe your leadership style? What is your leadership motivation?
As Dean of the College of Science, my primary responsibilities were designing and developing degree programs leading to international accreditation and creating a centre for excellence in teaching and research. A good leader must be a good listener and doer, and it is imperative to have a solid executive committee consisting of Heads of Departments, Assistant Deans, and the Director. They not only perform administrative duties but also play an advisory role. It is also essential to create an environment conducive to productive academic work and practice an open-door policy whereby all faculty and support staff have free access to the Dean. My leadership style is direct, and I lead by example.

What are the three things in life you are most proud of?
I would name my academic education and training, my teaching career at university, and my close-knit family. I can proudly proclaim that behind a successful woman, there is a supportive man! My husband and I have raised four beautiful children. During my career, I have been blessed with a string of 'firsts' some of which are: first Omani Head of the Department of Chemistry, first Omani to be promoted to Full Professor in the College of Science, first female Dean of the College of Science and first Omani to be appointed as a fellow of the prestigious organisation The World Academy of Science for the advancement of science in developing countries (TWAS).

What does it take to be a successful woman these days? What are the three top things successful business people should personalise?
Being highly organised to juggle work with family life, disciplined to follow a daily plan, and hardworking, as there is no shortcut to success. Accept constructive criticism and advice with grace. Delegate responsibilities to people who understand your dreams and can positively contribute to your work or business.

How would you describe yourself in three words?
If I were to describe myself in three words, I would say self-motivated, dedicated, and compassionate.

Samah Al Rawahi

What was the best piece of advice that you were given regarding your career and that you will never forget?

When I first started working, my father told me two things, "Always listen and don't get involved in politics". I never understood this until I started my career in the corporate world and began gaining experience and building my network. He taught me the importance of active listening, learning from the people around me, and never losing focus on my goals — the reasons why I am where I am today.

What has shaped you the most in your life? Is there any specific situation?

Twelve years ago, I set out to travel the longest from home, starting my college journey in America. Stepping onto that plane was one of the most exciting and, at the same time, frightening moments of my life. Despite my worries, I am forever grateful for my parents, who pushed me to get on that plane. My time abroad is one of the most rewarding. It gave me a new perspective on the world, helped me develop new passions, and taught me more about myself. Even more, it continues to inspire me to learn, grow, evolve, and explore the world for the rest of my life.

Who would you identify as your role model? Whom do you look up to and why?

As we experience life, we get inspired by the people we meet along the way. However, my parents are my most significant source of inspiration and my strongest supporters. I have learned from my father not to give up when anything gets tough and never be afraid to speak up my mind. My mother, the source of calm and confidence, taught me to know when to push hard and where to slow down.

What do you respect most in other successful women?

I respect women who venture to the unknown. Women who try to break the norms for the better, women who are change-makers, who accept and love themselves. Women who have the

External Communications & Brand Lead / Petroleum Development Oman

ability to harness their skills and embrace their weaknesses. Women who lift each other and inspire one another.

What would you recommend to a student just starting and dreaming of a successful career?
My most extensive advice to any student dreaming of a successful career is to be your true self and believe in your abilities to succeed. There is nothing impossible with hard work, determination, and a lifelong learner's mindset. It is essential to find something that you are passionate about, and only then can you flourish; with that said, not every job needs to address all your passions. Instead, use every job as an opportunity to learn and expand your network. Also, do not let failure scare you, instead learn from your mistakes. Lastly, do not wait for opportunities. Create them. Keep yourself motivated and work towards your dreams; options eventually pop up when you have a goal set and work on it.

If the entire world listened to you for five minutes, what would you say or what would you want to talk about?
Love yourself, believe in your ability to change and be the change you want to see in this world. The world is struggling with a significant presence of fear of those different from oneself. Now more than ever, we need authentic compassion. We need to be able to connect empathically with others. While I know this would not solve every crisis our world faces, many of these struggles would begin to dissolve around the globe.

How would you describe your leadership style? What is your leadership motivation?
I recently started leading a team virtually for the first time in the middle of a global pandemic. I know from experience that the most successful leaders are adaptable and flexible. Helping others and being able to inspire people is what motivates me the most. I make sure to invest time to listen and learn about their priorities, strengths and needs. I value their hard work and encourage them to take up challenges to reach their full potential while offering guidance and mentorship along the way.

Do you do anything to keep you fit physically or mentally, and how often?
I'm a firm believer in maintaining a balanced lifestyle and that my body is a temple. Physical activity does more than improve your physical health; it boosts your mood and reduces stress. I practice kickboxing at least three times a week, in which my love for this dynamic sport started three years ago. I try to stay active as much as I can and find opportunities to discover the hidden gems of Oman by organising and going on many hiking trips in which I habitually go with my sister and friends.

Is there a quote you favour that suits you? Or an important book you read that influenced you?
At the beginning of my career, I read a book called 'Lean In: Women, Work, and the Will to Lead' by Sheryl Sandberg. This book included many powerful messages that made me think harder and reflect on my behaviour as a woman in the workplace. The book left me feeling empowered, inspired and refreshed. I think it is a must-read not only for women but also for men in the workplace.

Samiya Al Balushi

What was the best piece of advice that you were given regarding your career and that you will never forget?
Venture outside your comfort zone and never stop learning.

What has shaped you the most in your life? Is there any specific situation?
I think the credit goes to my mentor, who believed in my capabilities and always granted me chances to shine in all aspects of my job. I was a person who wasn't able to speak in front of more than two people, and now I can facilitate any training, workshop or be a guest speaker in front of large groups.

On the path to where you are now, what was the most determining step?
Moving out of Oman for work, as I worked in Abu Dhabi, growing up in Omani Culture, was hard. However, my father believed in me and gave me this opportunity to showcase that Omani Women can work abroad to fulfil their dreams. They are equal to men.

Who would you identify as your role model? Whom do you look up to and why?
My father is my role model; he was the one I always looked up to since I was a child; he is a man with a vision and always strives for the best. And I have seen him grow in his career since he was very young. He always guided us with his advice, making us trust our own capabilities and never settle for less.

What do you respect most in other successful women?
Their dedication to their work while ensuring their lives are as successful as their work lives.
What would you recommend to a student just starting and dreaming of a successful career?
Have a clear goal and strive hard to achieve it.

Director of Human Resources / Jumeirah Muscat Bay

What are the three things in life you are most proud of?
My career, where I am today. Seeing my team members grow in their careers while joining my team as juniors, I know they lead teams. My two little talented girls.

What does it take to be a successful woman these days? What are the three top things successful business people should personalise?
Be yourself, set goals, learn, evolve, and one last thing is to accept "that you can't control everything".

The top 3 things are:
- Growth mindset
- Being self-motivated
- Taking risk

Is there a quote you favour that suits you? Or an important book you read that influenced you?
I believe in the below quotes I read:
"Your Smile is your logo".
"Your personality is your business card".
"How you leave others feeling after an experience with you becomes your trademark".

If you had extra time of four hours a day, what would you do during that time?
I would read more and ensure that I am upgrading my knowledge or spending time with my girls in an activity where we all learn something new.

How would you describe yourself in three words? Do you live with a daily routine and what is your secret to success?
No, my days are different every day; in HR in Hospitality, I always learn new things from other people I meet. I am creative, passionate, patient and approachable, and I like to create values for others.

Did the Omani culture you grew up in have an impact on your career path?
Women in Oman are given a chance to be equally important as men. They do contribute to the success of the country. The late Majesty Sultan Qaboos decided 17 October is celebrated every year as Omani Women's Day.

What is your favourite place in Oman, that you like to visit in order to relax and recharge your batteries?
The beaches in Oman are beautiful, and it provides positive energy. So when I feel drained, I visit the beaches. I feel recharged again with total positive energy.

Sara Fida

What was the best piece of advice that you were given regarding your career and that you will never forget?
One's comfort zone is a perilous place to be. Should a better opportunity arise, go for it.

What has shaped you the most in your life? Is there any specific situation?
The challenges I have faced, and stereotyping, gave me the determination to work even harder.

On the path to where you are now, what was the most determining step?
Diverting my career path from Graphic Design to Marketing was the best decision I have taken. Working as a graphic designer and art director at Ogilvy on a slew of international brands was extremely rewarding and a fantastic experience. After coming back to Oman, though, I still design daily, whether at work or as a freelancer.

Who would you identify as your role model? Whom do you look up to and why?
Strong women, in general, inspire me. Women who make headlines for their achievements and perseverance. Women who started from scratch and made a name for themselves and showed determination and patience every step of the way. As a physiotherapist dealing with kids with special needs, my mum showed us the meaning of kindness, patience, and compassion at a very young age. Zaha Hadid taught me that a woman could work her way up alone in a man's world. Jacinda Ardern taught me that leaders could be both empathetic and strong.

What do you respect most in other successful women?
I have the utmost respect for those who are dedicated and focussed on their goals, in total disregard for those doubting their merit.

What would you recommend to a student just starting and dreaming of a successful career?
Take risks. Don't let anyone make decisions for you. Take your own.

If the entire world listened to you for five minutes, what would you say or what would you want to talk about?
I would emphasise marketing and branding play a significant role in our daily life.

What essential qualifications do you think will be needed ten years from now?
Careers in technology and digital marketing.

How would you describe your leadership style? What is your leadership motivation?
Mentor or Coach-style leadership. I've learnt a lot during my years of experience. It's high time I paid it forward.

Head of Marketing & Communications / OMASCO – Honda

If there is a lot of work and you are under stress, how do you compensate?
I could always take a day off and unwind. Going to the beach or chilling at home can do the trick.

What are the three things in life you are most proud of?
Reaching where I am now on my career path. Buying a home at my age. Seeing where some PechaKucha Muscat speakers have reached after giving them the platform to speak about their inspiring work. That one occupies a special place in my heart.

Do you do anything to keep you fit physically or mentally, and how often?
Mentally: I take a break from social media every now and then. Physically: I go to the gym and enjoy hiking.

What does it take to be a successful woman these days? What are the three top things successful business people should personalise?
Self-belief, hard work, and dedication.

What would you devote your time and energy to if you were to invest now, in your future best self?
I would focus on networking with people in the same field to grow and gain more exposure abroad.
What are your most important goals? Is there a difference for you between life goals and career goals?
Yes, there's one.

But I guess it's more like a line in the sand, as they still influence each other. I want to travel a bit more and do more charity work, but with COVID-19, things have slowed down considerably. Career-wise, my goal is to become a CMO at a prestigious company.

How would you describe yourself in three words? Do you live with a daily routine, and what is your secret to success?
Being kind, ambitious, and creative. My curiosity and passion make me successful in my field. I ask a lot and read quite a bit, too, not books, but online articles, because marketing is so fast-paced and constantly evolving that books just can't catch up with it.

(Dr.) Sausan Al Riyami

What was the best piece of advice that you were given regarding your career and that you will never forget?
During your career path journey, you often need to decide between fun and hard work, various sacrifices are expected and required. Enjoying what you are doing will help you to balance it.

What has shaped you the most in your life? Is there any specific situation?
Family. They support, inspire, and motivate me in various directions and encourage me to discover the world through reading.

What would you recommend to a student just starting and dreaming of a successful career?
Not to limit themselves with what they learn or know from school or universities. However, they should continually expand their knowledge since a successful career path needs patience, hard work, and dreaming about it.

If the entire world listened to you for five minutes, what would you say or what would you want to talk about?
The meaning of success! Success comes in different shapes and scales. Therefore, people should appreciate their lives and think about their success stories based on their achievements and not others' judgment.

How would you describe your leadership style? What is your leadership motivation?
Leadership has several styles, each with its own benefits and challenges. In my opinion, mixing between the types depending on the situation, environment, culture, organisation's goal, and the team will be, in many cases, necessary. It needs balancing each time. You will realise that you are building your leadership style representing 'yourself' rather than someone else in this process.

If there is a lot of work and you are under stress, how do you compensate?
With so much work and stress, I usually make sure not to unnecessarily rush making critical decisions. Instead, I tend to face the challenge, prioritise the tasks, and draw a time management matrix that I usually apply to achieve deadlines and high deliverables.

Do you do anything to keep you fit physically or mentally, and how often?
I usually prefer to walk and read various books or articles on multiple topics or watch a documentary.

Is there a quote you favour that suits you? Or an important book you read that influenced you?
"A bird does not build a nest in a cage so that its son does not inherit slavery!!"
by Gibran Khalil Gibran.

Also, "As the saying goes, the Stone Age did not end because we ran out of stones; we transitioned to better solutions. The same opportunity lies before us with energy efficiency and clean energy", by Steven Chu.

If you had extra time of four hours a day, what would you do during that time?
Spend it with my family! Also, I would read additional pages from a new book.

What is your favourite place in Oman, that you like to visit in order to relax and recharge your batteries?
For me, it is usually at home with family and a walk on one of the great Muscat beaches.

"People should appreciate their lives and think about their success stories based on their achievements and not others' judgment"

Shadha Al Raisi

What was the best piece of advice that you were given regarding your career and that you will never forget?
Take one day at a time. A piece of advice I received from a friend during my time studying medicine in Ireland. It helped reassure me to take every challenge of every day as they come. Today I remind myself to "Just keep moving forward". At times, there may be slow days in terms of what you have accomplished, but even these tiny accomplishments help you climb that ladder of personal success and growth.

What has shaped you the most in your life? Is there any specific situation?
The ups and downs in a 10-year journey away from the comfort of family and home while studying abroad. I was very fortunate to have had a circle of close friends from different nationalities who were my support system and helped guide me. I learnt how diverse the world was. We all have something to teach one another, and our cultures shape our stories.

Who would you identify as your role model? Whom do you look up to and why?
I try to learn from every person I meet. I have had a very positive influence within my family. While watching my father and my husband, I picked up a high work ethic and perseverance. My older sister is an actual role model in her determination and commitment to her career and family. I learnt from my late mother that your intentions in every aspect of your life must be pure. I am very fortunate that my intentions for all work could be as simple as to help provide care to those in need.

What do you respect most in other successful women?
Dedication and determination which does not always come easy in a male-dominated world. It is easy to lose focus when you are trying to build up a career and look after your family at the same time. It is also very easy to be put off by negative comments and criticism. But I admire the persistence and determination that I see in many of my female colleagues and friends.

What would you recommend to a student just starting and dreaming of a successful career?
Set a goal and make sure you dream big, aim high and enjoy the journey with all its ups and downs. Throughout the years, I have learnt to stretch myself to the limit. To take on all opportunities and challenges. I advise everyone to take advantage of different opportunities. To avoid saying no to opportunities, even what may seem minor or challenging at the time. But rather to see how strong they become once they put themselves in situations that could only make them grow.

How would you describe your leadership style? What is your leadership motivation?
The source of my motivation comes from the team in the department and knowing that the work we do directly affects healthcare providers in the health facilities and patients. They will end up receiving the training, the medications, and the treatment they need. A goal worth waking up to every morning. I hope I am seen as practising a cohesive and collaborative leadership

Director of Non-Communicable Diseases / Ministry of Health Oman

style. I believe the role of the leader is to set the vision and that common goal the team would need to strive for. I try to ensure transparency, encourage the sharing of ideas and emphasise the value of teamwork.

If there is a lot of work and you are under stress, how do you compensate?
There are weeks where everything is urgent; then, I try to set priorities. Also, delegating is essential — making sure that at least part of this stress is shared amongst the team. I believe this is important not only to reduce the pressure on the leader but also to give the team a chance to grow, learn, and be recognised.

What does it take to be a successful woman these days? What are the three top things successful business people should personalise?
Be persistent. Aim high. Every one of us needs to know that the sky's the limit to what we can achieve. Never be intimidated, and don't have self-doubt.

What would you devote your time and energy to if you were to invest now, in your future best self?
My children and my mental wellbeing. I have learnt of late that my mental health is as important as my physical health. So I have now been actively trying to make sure that I am firm in my thoughts and react positively in different situations.

What are your most important goals? Is there a difference for you between life goals and career goals?
I am fortunate that my line of work involves providing services and care for those in need. My work goal is to continue to ensure the sustainable provision of health services to patients. In addition, my life goal is to develop a strong family and ensure that my kids grow up to be capable adults.

What is your favourite place in Oman, that you like to visit in order to relax and recharge your batteries?
My family loves to be on the boat at sea. We snorkel, dive and swim and create the most precious of memories together.

Shadya Al Ismaily

What was the best piece of advice that you were given regarding your career and that you will never forget?

During the early days of my career, I worked under a great inspiring leader who cultivated employees' empowerment and recognition at the workplace. As a result, for me, going to the office every morning was fun and fulfilling. Having recognised the power of these values, I committed to nurturing, enabling and empowering members of any team that I would manage. Naturally, the impact was leading motivated, creative, and dedicated teams with outstanding results.

On the path to where you are now, what was the most determining step?
2008 was a turning point in my career. I felt that my work reached a stage where it no longer fulfilled my aspirations. I thought of giving it a few years; maybe things will improve. Meanwhile, my daughter Suad and I started setting up our brand "Deema". Three years passed, nothing changed, and my passion for designing got even more substantial. I became possessed by designing; to an extent, I started transforming anything I looked at into a beautiful jewellery design. In 2011, I resigned, which meant giving up on a guaranteed and decent monthly salary, with no pension to enjoy down the line. However, I trusted it was worthwhile focusing on "Deema" and doing something I love and enjoy most.

What would you recommend to a student just starting and dreaming of a successful career?
I would say to them that to be a successful person, it is not necessary to be a doctor, an engineer, an accountant, or a lawyer. You will be successful if you are passionate, enjoy, and committed to what you do.

Once you have determined what you are passionate about, have a clear vision of what you want to do and where you wish to take it to; have a business plan, implement it and evaluate your performance very frequently. Surround yourself with positive people and do not take 'No' for an answer. You cannot be an expert in all fields, so seek help in areas you lack expertise. Finally, self-development is crucial, so keep learning.

If the entire world listened to you for five minutes, what would you say or what would you want to talk about?
Importance of diversity and inclusiveness in peacebuilding, security, and development of the world.

Founder & CEO / DEEMA - Luxury Design Brand

What essential qualifications do you think will be needed ten years from now?
The creative industry is considered one of the most rapidly growing sectors of the world economy. According to UNESCO, the world trade of creative goods and services recorded US$624 billion in 2011. This tells a lot! When we talk about the creative industry or economy, it includes audio-visual products, design, media, performing arts, and publishing and visual arts. In addition, technology is another vital area.

How would you describe your leadership style? What is your leadership motivation?
I believe my leadership style is more of a combination of coach-style and transformational leadership. I strongly encourage having the right people in the right places. So, when building a team, I make sure that each team member is given a role that is in line with their area of expertise or skill set. I share with them the vision that I have for the team and make sure that each of them contributes to the execution plan. Then, I do whatever it takes to keep them motivated and empowered to achieve our goals.

What are the three things in life you are most proud of?
My family; The value I added to each organisation that I worked for; Building a luxury brand from scratch known for its high standards; attracted many and is recognised locally and internationally.

What does it take to be a successful woman these days? What are the three top things successful business people should personalise?
My recipe for success is passion, focus, positiveness, influential network, dedication, and delegation.

If you had extra time of four hours a day, what would you do during that time?
In addition to daily physical exercising, I would sign up for a pottery class with my grandchildren. Thus, I would be hitting two birds with one stone: enjoying quality time with them while learning a new hobby.

How would you describe yourself in three words? Do you live with a daily routine, and what is your secret to success?
Unfortunately, yes, and this sometimes may sound like I'm missing out on some social fun! My day starts at 4 am, doing various things ranging from spiritual to spending time with my family and working at Deema and then ending my day on a couch in my quiet living room, watching a light movie.

Since I worked in both the public and private sectors, I must say that achieving one's aspirations in any field is impossible without a clear vision, proper research, and a comprehensive plan. I am very determined, focused, and result-oriented as an entrepreneur; I never give up easily. Moreover, I am credible and take advantage of constructive feedback.

(Dr.) Shamsa Al Sheibani

What was the best piece of advice that you were given regarding your career and that you will never forget?
Believe in yourself and stay positive. Remember that the sky's the limit. Never give up. This is what I advised myself.

On the path to where you are now, what was the most determining step?
The most crucial step that I now face is overcoming the glass ceiling and glass cliff, two concepts I have recently realised that exist in real life.

Who would you identify as your role model? Whom do you look up to and why?
There is no specific role model that I look up to. Instead, I admire determined and successful people who have a strong mission and vision in all aspects of their lives.

What do you respect most in other successful women?
I respect most of their passion and resilience in achieving their mission by balancing their work and social lives without compromising their feminist nature.

What would you recommend to a student just starting and dreaming of a successful career?
I will recommend the student to read, read and read. Reading takes us to a world of the impossible, a world full of wonders, creativity, and opportunities.

If the entire world listened to you for five minutes, what would you say or what would you want to talk about?
Life is too short and fragile, so handle it with care. Remember why we exist, what we need to do and how to reach peacefully to our destination.

How would you describe your leadership style? What is your leadership motivation?
I am leading by example. I am motivated by believing that work is obedience. Therefore, we should perform it with passion and faithfulness.

If there is a lot of work and you are under stress, how do you compensate?
When there is a lot of work and stress at the workplace, I reward myself with a package in my favourite SPA, do shopping, and watch an aspirational movie.

Vice President-Economics Research / OMINVEST

What are the three things in life you are most proud of?
I am proud of my country for being a peaceful destination for all humankind now and throughout history. I am proud of my family for being lovable, supportive, and understanding. Finally, I am proud of myself for being me despite all the challenges that I face in my life.

Do you do anything to keep you fit physically or mentally, and how often?
I love walking outside in the natural fields, which I do on average five times a week. I also like the beautiful nature: gardens, beaches, mountains, wadis, and deserts. In addition, I generally like to meditate, pray, and imagine.

What does it take to be a successful woman these days? What are the three top things successful business people should personalise?
It takes hope, determination, resilience, and positiveness for a woman to be successful not only today but always. The top three things successful business people should personalise are their vision, mission, and strategic plans.

What would you devote your time and energy to if you were to invest now, in your future best self?
I will put my time and energy into working on the optimal mix or the right formula in all aspects of my life, where win-win situations exist.

What are your most important goals? Is there a difference for you between life goals and career goals?
My personal goal is to maintain a peaceful and healthy life full of joy and happiness. My career goal is to reach higher heights, somewhere at the peak successfully.

How would you describe yourself in three words? Do you live with a daily routine?
Yes, I can say that I live within a daily routine in the circle of four primary particles: home, prayer, work, and leisure. I would describe myself as thoughtful, lovable, and ambitious.

Did the Omani culture you grew up in have an impact on your career path?
Yes, the Omani culture that I grew up in has impacted my career path by having the correct values: integrity, excellence, good citizenship, collaboration, and creativity.

What is your favourite place in Oman, that you like to visit in order to relax and recharge your batteries?
There is no favourite place. I like every bit of Oman! However, I want to watch the sunrise and sunset. I also like to walk when it rains, and I like to see the rainbow, birds, and shooting stars.

Sharifa Al Harthy

What was the best piece of advice that you were given regarding your career and that you will never forget?
Put yourself in the shoes of others. Understand the circumstances of others and always judge fairly.

What has shaped you the most in your life? Is there any specific situation?
I was born in Zanzibar to a wealthy Omani Arab family; my grandfather was the paramount Sheik president of the Arabs in Zanzibar. In 1964, when I was nine years old, there was a violent revolution that stripped all the Arabs of their possessions and properties. My family had to immigrate first to Saudi Arabia, Kuwait, and then UAE before coming back to Oman. We had nothing with us; everything was taken away. However, we had our principles. We had to rebuild ourselves. My parents struggled to educate us. They taught us important principles such as honesty, integrity, self-dependence and the value of education and hard work. That is the only thing no one can take away from you.

On the path to where you are now, what was the most determining step?
I decided to go to the US to do my masters. At the time, I had four children. Taking my children with me was extremely hard. I had to manage between my studies and taking care of my family as a single parent as my husband had to manage his business in Oman.

Who would you identify as your role model? Whom do you look up to and why?
My role model is my husband; I was with him when he started his business from scratch. He believes in fairness, recognises others' hard work, transparency, and informs his employees on what is happening regardless of whether it's good or bad.

What do you respect most in other successful women?
Intelligence and determination. It isn't easy for a woman to be highly ranked.

What would you recommend to a student just starting and dreaming of a successful career?
First of all, your education is number one, but first, you should know what you want to do. Read many things outside of your studies: general knowledge of science, art, finance, marketing, etc.

If the entire world listened to you for five minutes, what would you say or what would you want to talk about?
Respect, peace and fairness to others. Being able to recognise, accept, and apologise when you are wrong. The importance of education and working hard.

What essential qualifications do you think will be needed ten years from now?
Flexibility, meaning changing your direction and adapting to the new environment and trends

MBF Chairperson

as the world is changing quickly. Being cosmopolitan, to work in harmony with different people with different backgrounds, ethnicity and religions.

How would you describe your leadership style? What is your leadership motivation?
I have an open-door policy where people can talk to me if they have any issues. I have compassion for others; I recognise and encourage their efforts and achievements.

What are the three things in life you are most proud of?
I'm proud of my family, my achievements and our charity foundation. Being able to give back and smile at others who are less fortunate gives me satisfaction and happiness.

Which topics should humanity focus more on in the future?
Humanities and sociology. I think if we all understood people better, the world would be a more peaceful place.

What are the three top things successful business people should personalise?
Education, hard work and learning from your mistakes.

What would you devote your time and energy to if you were to invest now, in your future
best self?
Reading and learning about different cultures and religions.

Is there a quote you favour that suits you? Or an important book you read that influenced you?
Treat others how you want to be treated.

What are your most important goals? Is there a difference for you between life goals and career goals?
Helping others and giving back to the community. Giving back isn't just about spending money. Sometimes they need someone to listen to them and advise them.

How would you describe yourself in three words? Do you live with a daily routine?
Wake up, exercise, then work.
In three words, I am outgoing, socially active, and quickly adapt and fit in anywhere.

Shatha Salim Al Maskiry

What was the best piece of advice that you were given regarding your career and that you will never forget?
A senior female partner at PwC said: "To excel in consultancy, you need to ask all the right questions that will encourage the client to do all the talking. You should be able to identify at least three challenges or pain areas they are facing which you can help them solve".

What has shaped you the most in your life? Is there any specific situation?
My younger brother's early departure from life made me reassess my priorities, starting with my family and ending with serving humanity. However, we must put ourselves first if we want the world to meet our best selves. Unexpected events help you realise that we should count our every blessing from the air we breathe to the good night's sleep we get.

Who would you identify as your role model? Whom do you look up to and why?
My beloved mother, who was a strict disciplinarian, and my mentor today. She showered us with an abundance of love and innate compassion. I follow her rock-solid belief: we are obliged to serve one another to the best of our abilities with grace and gratitude.

What do you respect most in other successful women?
A successful woman is both passionate and principled. She knows what she wants and desires to positively impact other people's lives. Success is being honest with ourselves, confident in speaking our minds, knowing what, when, and how to say it, and carving out ways to navigate challenges with our unique feminine energy. Most importantly, to do it all unapologetically and with mental resilience.

What would you recommend to a student just starting and dreaming of a successful career?
There is no fixed definition for success. Don't give power to others to define it for you. Ultimately, the most significant part of success is doing what you love, what you are good at, what energises you, and what inspires you to seize the day. Take the time to explore yourself, and then go ahead and do what is meaningful and fulfilling for you to shine in your most glorious light.

What essential qualifications do you think will be needed ten years from now?
The only qualification that will never expire is being a 'continuous learner', as no qualification or degree will amount to it. I believe there will be a significant focus on innovation, personal branding, problem-solving, critical thinking, emotional intelligence, and the ability to learn and adapt quickly.

How would you describe your leadership style? What is your leadership motivation?
I got shaped into a situational leader due to my consulting career as I work with different generations, calibres, and nationalities. Depending on the profile, I am either guiding, delegating, coaching, or training them, depending on their professional maturity, competence, and

Managing Director / Protiviti

commitment. I am also constantly adjusting based on the needs; some need rules and guidelines, some need inspiration, some prefer teaming and brainstorming, and others want to be empowered so they can drive their own career.

What does it take to be a successful woman these days? What are the three top things successful business people should personalise?

As we experience the fourth industrial revolution, success requires women to have a strong sense of self-belief, confidence, and determination to succeed according to their own terms. "If you think you can, you can. If you think you can't, you're right!" They should know what their authentic personal brand is and remain relevant and innovative. Smart women keep learning and developing themselves, and when it is coupled with their passion and persistence, their work will stand the test of time.

Is there a quote you favour that suits you? Or an important book you read that influenced you?

Three books that opened my eyes and heart were "The Celestine Prophecy" by James Redfield, "Ishmael" by Daniel Quinn and "The seven people you meet in Heaven" by Mitch Albom. These books cover a broad spectrum of perspectives on humanity, ego, control, and judgment. It will make you think deeply about beliefs, expand your views of the world, and appreciate the beauty of humanity.

How would you describe yourself in three words? Do you live with a daily routine, and what is your secret to success?

No day is a routine for me, and as a business consultant, I am inspired by the unknowns and the challenges that come with it as we are constantly stimulated to solve problems.

Did the Omani culture you grew up in have an impact on your career path?

Omanis have natural competitive advantages; among them is humility, hospitality, and moderation. We are also open and accepting, which can be attributed to our geography and sea-faring history.

Shemsa Al-Nabhani

What was the best piece of advice that you were given regarding your career and that you will never forget?
"Don't work hard, work smart".

What has shaped you the most in your life? Is there any specific situation?
We all go through challenging experiences in our lives, and though at the time it didn't seem easy, I believe everything happens for a good reason. Later, things presented themselves as blessings in disguise. It all depends on perception and patience. My childhood and marriage life experiences have moulded me into the person I am today.

Who would you identify as your role model? Whom do you look up to and why?
Most definitely my mother. I cannot express enough how much I look up to her and have learned many life lessons. She is also my best friend and is the reason for me reaching this far in life.

If the entire world listened to you for five minutes, what would you say or what would you want to talk about?
The most significant illnesses in the world today are hatred and greed. People have suffered far too much for far too long because of it. We need to put aside all differences, egos, and personal agendas and start spreading love, respect, and kindness. There is more than enough to go around for everyone.

What essential qualifications do you think will be needed ten years from now?
The best and most valuable superpowers and qualifications to possess are common sense and emotional intelligence. People should not be judged only by their educational status but more on the intellect of the mind and heart. If you have both, you can excel in whatever career path you choose. Emotional intelligence is crucial.

Marketing Communications Officer / Oman Air
Psychologist / Whispers of Serenity Clinic

How would you describe your leadership style? What is your leadership motivation?
The best way to lead is to listen more than you talk and give more than you take. People don't need to be instructed on what to do; they need proper guidance, positivity, and motivation. Let people make their own decisions.

If there is a lot of work and you are under stress, how do you compensate?
Balance in work and mental health is vital. There is no point in trying to fill a cup that is already full. Whenever I feel that I need to release, my therapy has always been art and music.

What are the three things in life you are most proud of?
- My parents
- My children
- My achievements and ability to offer help to others

Do you do anything to keep you fit physically or mentally, and how often?
From a young age, I have always been engaged in different kinds of sport. I have always loved to keep physically active. The best way to maintain a healthy mind is to love and laugh a lot. It's the best therapy.

Which topics should humanity focus more on in the future?
Mental health. The mind is more powerful than most people presume, and it holds the key to curing most illnesses.

What would you devote your time and energy to if you were to invest now, in your future best self?
Keep your circle small and focus on who matters most. For me, the family has always been number one. Invest your time and energy in yourself first, those who truly matter and situations you can control.

What are your most important goals? Is there a difference for you between life goals and career goals?
My goal is to raise my children as best I can by teaching them the best life principles. I also aspire to one day have a more significant influence to touch and impact more on people's lives and reach higher authority to change or make global decisions.

What is your favourite place in Oman, that you like to visit in order to relax and recharge your batteries?
One of my favourite places to connect with my true self, find peace and relax, is the beautiful village of Tanuf, which is nestled in Nizwa province. My father's family originated from there, and some of my favourite memories of growing up there were especially during the Eid holidays where the family gathered. I prefer small-town life more than city life. Being out in nature has always been a preference for me, as it is stress-relieving.

Sora Al Rowas (MD, MSc)

What has shaped you the most in your life? Is there any specific situation?
In my profession, as well as the various countries I have lived in, I was exposed to a broad spectrum of human suffering and hardship. This perspective has reminded me to always be grateful and to foster greater compassion for what people might be going through instead of wrongly assuming that a good work ethic is all it takes to succeed in life.

What do you respect most in other successful women?
I have great respect and admiration for women with strong personalities. I have direct experience of how much scrutiny women receive, especially in leadership positions. A woman who is frank and open about who she is, regardless of circumstances, is someone I always want to support and uplift.

What would you recommend to a student just starting and dreaming of a successful career?
Young people are preparing for a world whose parameters remain unclear. We need the dreamers and the thinkers to maintain their freedom of thought to shape the future, not just fit into someone else's box. I would tell them not to be afraid of taking time off to travel and grow. They can benefit from broadening their horizons and taking time to understand who they are.

If the entire world listened to you for five minutes, what would you say or what would you want to talk about?
I wish everyone in the world would spend time evaluating their beliefs and ask themselves: "Is there something in my belief system that dehumanises other people? How can I live with more compassion for others and myself?"

What essential qualifications do you think will be needed ten years from now?
There will be less focus on degrees and more focus on competence. Competency-based assessment has already revolutionised medical training and has been integral to high-risk industries like aviation. Lifetime learners who remain flexible and adaptable will be the ones most poised for success in a new world.

How would you describe your leadership style? What is your leadership motivation?
I think it is important that everyone on a team understands the team's purpose and how each activity fits into the greater mission and vision. This helps each member better respond to situations that may come up and facilitate valuable communication. Building redundancy for essential tasks is also extremely important to ensure work continues, even if a member is unavailable. I call this an 'understanding centred' approach.

If there is a lot of work and you are under stress, how do you compensate?
A high cognitive load decreases our capacity to make good decisions. It also reduces our ability to effectively regulate emotions. Bringing mindfulness to each moment helps in maintaining excellence, even under pressure. Ironically, working slower is the best way to deal with a

Internal Medicine Consultant & Educator /Al Sorat Consulting

heavy workload because it decreases the chance of stress-induced error. Scheduling rest time strategically throughout the day also dramatically increases our efficiency and productivity.

What are the three things in life you are most proud of?
I have had various successes in my life. Rather than career milestones, I am most proud of the intentional personal growth I dedicated time to. It was important to me to maintain my compassion and ethics regardless of the pressures of my career to make those secondary.

Do you do anything to keep you fit physically or mentally, and how often?
Yoga has changed my life. I do my best to practise every day, and this brings me great peace and joy. The infinite journey inwards has been more exciting than any of my travels. My other great medicine is to be out in nature. Nothing brings perspective to a situation like a horizon.

What does it take to be a successful woman these days? What are the three top things successful business people should personalise?
It is important to be able to bounce back from a fall. Women are judged a lot more harshly than men, and it is important to build resilience to perceived failure and have the strength to get up and try again when things don't go well. Developing close friendships with other women, a sisterhood is key to help us stay upright when the world rocks beneath our feet.

What would you devote your time and energy to if you were to invest now, in your future best self?
I highly suggest that each person spends time focusing on the inner self; understanding who you are allows you to make better decisions. Make time for hobbies that develop the mind and the body - we are replaceable anywhere, but our mind and body are the only home we really have.

What are your most important goals? Is there a difference for you between life goals and career goals?
There is a massive difference for me. I used to be very focused on career milestones. The past few years have radically shifted my priorities towards meaning and community rather than titles and awards. My life goal is to empower people and institutions to become the best versions of themselves.

How would you describe yourself in three words? Do you live with a daily routine, and what is your secret to success?
Happiness is a success. The key to happiness is to radically forgive oneself and others. It is also celebrating positive movements, no matter how small. Our inner voice is the one that shapes our destiny. We can use it to uplift and empower ourselves or to diminish ourselves with criticism. Choose wisely.

Suad Al Balushi

What was the best piece of advice that you were given regarding your career and that you will never forget?
Focus, focus, focus! Always be ready for the next opportunity through acquiring the skills and knowledge required; you never know when the next opening is coming up.

What has shaped you the most in your life? Is there any specific situation?
There is no single factor, but multiple factors shaped my personality in general. Being the eldest among my sisters gave me the advantage of taking up the lead on many occasions. I always believe there is nothing impossible; if someone has done it, you can do it.

On the path to where you are now, what was the most determining step?
I was moving out of my comfort zone and joining my current organisation. First, it wasn't easy to move out of my previous organisation after 14 years, but after joining, I realised there is a lot to do and contribute outside of my comfort zone.

Who would you identify as your role model? Whom do you look up to and why?
There is no single role model, but I look up to many people for different aspects of life.

What do you respect most in other successful women?
Their dedication, sacrifice, commitment and how they are managing their work-life balance.
What would you recommend to a student just starting and dreaming of a successful career?
Learn as much as you can and differentiate yourself through getting professional qualifications or acquiring specific skills. Always question why you are doing what you are doing. Maybe you are more thoughtful and can do it in a better way. Never doubt your abilities!

What essential qualifications do you think will be needed ten years from now?
I believe social and emotional intelligence and digital literacy are essential qualifications ten years from now. This is because social media and technology, in general, changed how we communicate or socialise and conduct business.

How would you describe your leadership style? What is your leadership motivation?
I believe in collaborative leadership and bringing the best out of people is my motive.

If there is a lot of work and you are under stress, how do you compensate?
I prepare my "to-do" list, where part of it is to have a break with my family and friends.

Do you do anything to keep you fit physically or mentally, and how often?
Health is the most important gift in life because you can't do or enjoy anything without good health. Hence, physical and mental health are key to me. I wake up early, do regular exercises but not heavy ones, eat healthy most of the time and practice my hobbies.

Head of Global Markets / Bank Nizwa

Which topics should humanity focus more on in the future?
We are still facing global warming, which needs more attention; I believe environmental sustainability to protect global ecosystems is one. Another focus area would be the education system, in general, which needs more attention globally.

What does it take to be a successful woman these days? What are the three top things successful business people should personalise?
Competition is intense nowadays. Hence, it is crucial to differentiate yourself and have your brand equity. The second would be time management and getting the most out of your time. The third aspect would be that planning and prioritisation are crucial to getting things done; don't leave it for coincidences.

Is there a quote you favour that suits you? Or an important book you read that influenced you?
A quote that suits me is the old African proverb, "If you educate a man, you educate an individual, but if you educate a woman, you educate a family (nation)". Oman has done great in achieving this by giving both men and women equal opportunities to build and contribute to the nation.

One of the books that I encourage parents and educators to read is "Prepared: What kids need for a fulfilled life" by Diane Tavenner. It gives a blueprint on how parents can stop worrying about their children's future instead, helping them prepare for it.

What is your favourite place in Oman, that you like to visit in order to relax and recharge your batteries?
One of my favourite places is Jabal al Akhdar, which is part of Al Hajar Mountain. Usually, the weather is cooler than in other parts of Oman. Escaping on top of the mountains with fresh and clean air, having a local harvest, and interacting with nature is relaxing.

Sukainah Abdullah

What was the best piece of advice that you were given regarding your career and that you will never forget?

One of my managers once said to me: "Growth happens outside your comfort zone". Since then, this has always been a trigger. At the end of the day, I sit back and reflect. How was my day? Were there any challenges today? If it looks pretty smooth, I will look for a more challenging day ahead. This will either help me in improving an existing skill or learn something new.

Who would you identify as your role model? Whom do you look up to and why?

My grandfather, Abdullah Sulaiman Al Lawati, is one of the role models I always looked up to. He was self-driven, self-made, and he always made people-centric decisions. I have heard many stories about him that encourage me to look around and see what changes I may apply.

What would you recommend to a student just starting and dreaming of a successful career?

"If you can dream it, you can do it" - Walt Disney. Be ambitious. Please do what you are good at; make sure you do it with passion. Only then you will see fruitful results. Others expect 110% from you; make sure you deliver 120%.

If the entire world listened to you for five minutes, what would you say or what would you want to talk about?

Everything is temporary; make sure you spend every second of your life making the best decisions that will be best for you. Prioritization changes with time; it is only you who can know what is best for you. Be generous, kind, and listen. Think ahead of just you. When you have a positive thinking mindset, you will gradually think of your surroundings and improve them.

What essential qualifications do you think will be needed ten years from now?

I think there should be a bigger focus on enhancing the education system. Technology and

Head of Payments and Cash Management / Oman Arab Bank

Innovation are the way forward. Artificial Intelligence will be further introduced in various industries. But, of course, we will always need the traditional wisdom to work hand in hand with creativity.

How would you describe your leadership style? What is your leadership motivation?
I am probably more of a transformational leader; I always look for individual potentials and help that individual to bring those skills to the team. I lead by example. I believe people learn faster when they see the job being done. Allow others to aspire to achieve higher goals. I am proud of my direct approach, which saves time, energy and eliminates any ambiguity.

Which topics should humanity focus more on in the future?
The rapid changes that have taken place lately have impacted how we should shift our vision from the traditional concepts to tech visions. We have become technology-centric. With this, we will need to include these changes in the way we manage. Therefore, the leadership approaches should be adaptive to the innovation culture.

What does it take to be a successful woman these days? What are the three top things successful business people should personalise?
Willing to take risks to explore uncharted fields, unlearning the decaying skills and acquiring up-to-date knowledge and skills, and dedicate time and effort.

Is there a quote you favour that suits you? Or an important book you read that influenced you?
"Great things in business are never done by one person; they are done by a team of people" - Steve Jobs. Therefore, I favour group work, as I believe everyone will have a particular skill contributing to the common goal.

What are your most important goals? Is there a difference for you between life goals and career goals?
I will choose to be knowledgeable and ensure that I keep growing my knowledge in various areas that will add up to my life and career goals and maintain a work-life balance.

Did the Omani culture you grew up in have an impact on your career path?
I always appreciate in the Omani culture that people are down to earth and will always have a helping hand to offer. I truly admire it, and it is embedded within me as a person.

What is your favourite place in Oman, that you like to visit in order to relax and recharge your batteries?
Oman is a beautiful country; there are many places I enjoy. My favourite place is Al Jabal Al Akhdar with its beautiful mountains and fantastic climate. I enjoy hiking trails, and it has lovely paths to explore.

Sumaiya Al Wahaibi

What was the best piece of advice that you were given regarding your career and that you will never forget?
On my 25th birthday, a friend told me, "Life is so much bigger than a man or a woman; take that academic abroad opportunity!" I very much took that to heart; I spent years after that living happily in my suitcase.

What has shaped you the most in your life? Is there any specific situation?
There were many situations; however, choosing to be a researcher on women's studies and constantly meeting other women from around the world has shaped my life experience drastically. In the last few years, I volunteered with more than six civil entities in different development programmes in Turkey, Poland, the UK, Sri Lanka, Lebanon, and Oman related to gender and education. Throughout these projects, I had the chance to work with people from more than 45 different countries.

On the path to where you are now, what was the most determining step?
To study and work/volunteer abroad for years is the most decisive step. The international exposure has prepared me to be an innovative problem solver with always a global perspective. Moreover, it equipped me with solid confidence to work with multinational teams while considering their intersectional ties.

What do you respect most in other successful women?
To always try to help other women to succeed and to let other successful people shine, too.
What would you recommend to a student just starting and dreaming of a successful career?
Don't believe there is a box where you should cater your thoughts, as the journey to truly knowing yourself starts now! Embrace yourself and never stop learning and growing! A growth mindset, instead of a flexible one, would take you to so many places. Know yourself, your worth, and how to manage your energy well.

What essential qualifications do you think will be needed ten years from now?
Higher educational degrees in data & AI sciences. Also, qualifications related to human subjective well being.

How would you describe your leadership style? What is your leadership motivation?
I try to lead from the heart. As I mainly work with young professionals, it is always essential to make them feel valued and seen; therefore, letting them shine is fundamental to my leadership style. Moreover, it changes the power dynamics of the team positively.

If there is a lot of work and you are under stress, how do you compensate?
I would take a break, rest, and enjoy my time doing nothing! I always meet my deadlines and rarely miss deadlines in my professional life. It is essential for me that I don't force myself. Instead, I consciously give myself permission to rest and do anything else.

International Relations Specialist / UNESCO-NATCOM

Which topics should humanity focus more on in the future?
I wish to see less talking about gender equality and equity and a more fruitful focus on thriving as equal partners in our societies. I hope people can move on from focusing on the trivial.

What would you devote your time and energy to if you were to invest now, in your future best self?
Education, education, and education!

Is there a quote you favour that suits you? Or an important book you read that influenced you?
"You can't lose if you never quit" is my favourite motto. It tells you how determined most of the time I am!

What are your most important goals? Is there a difference for you between life goals and career goals?
Yes, there is a difference, career-wise. My current goal is to gain a steady income without having to overwork myself. Also, to have a balanced work and personal life. While my main life goal this year was to have a home of my own, which I finally got a few months ago!

How would you describe yourself in three words? Do you live with a daily routine, and what is your secret to success?
I don't particularly appreciate committing to a routine, but a list of things helps me stay sane, such as volunteering for a cherished cause, enjoying a hearty meal, and quality time with my family and close friends. I would describe myself as a caring, passionate, and devoted human being. What makes me successful is my high level of determination. I don't wish for things to happen, but I instead make it happen!

Did the Omani culture you grew up in have an impact on your career path?
Certainly! Growing in a society full of Do's and Don not's lists of appropriate things for young girls to do and the most suitable professions for women made me choose to break the ceilings and be a gender specialist instead.

What is your favourite place in Oman, that you like to visit in order to relax and recharge your batteries?
Misfat Al Abriyeen, and Al Jabal Al Sharqi.

Taghreed Al Lawati

What was the best piece of advice that you were given regarding your career and that you will never forget?
Do your best and keep the rest on Allah. Then, the doors will open for you. I was also given a similar piece of advice in my early career: do your best and don't accept an immediate return. You have to let people see your efforts and the change you make.

What has shaped you the most in your life? Is there any specific situation?
I studied at the University of Denton in Texas after high school. Studying abroad is a different experience as one has to come out of the comfort zone and family shelter. It teaches various social, communication and even survival skills. I am thankful to my family, and especially my dad, who supported me in studying overseas. I was the first girl in my family who went on a scholarship to the USA and moved to the UK to complete my degree.

What do you respect most in other successful women?
I respect the will we have as women. Overcoming the challenges that a woman faces: starting from work-life balance, being a wife and mom who wants to give the best to her family and beloved kids, being a daughter, sister etc., at the same time wanting to do the best at work.
What would you recommend to a student just starting and dreaming of a successful career?
Learn as much as possible from colleagues around you with passion and love. Don't expect an immediate return for everything you do. Good work pays later when people get to know you more, and your achievements talk about themselves.

If the entire world listened to you for five minutes, what would you say or what would you want to talk about?
I would speak about my beloved country, Oman. I am so proud of being Omani. I was born and grew up in the capital, blessed with the best education I had in government school till grade 9. Then I got a scholarship to private school and then to study abroad. In Oman, there is respect for every culture and tradition; it feels like one family wherever you go in Oman.

What essential qualifications do you think will be needed ten years from now?
I believe the ethical values and social skills students learn during school and university are crucial in how they perform in the workplace. Technology and data analytics will be more focused, but the traditional qualifications will remain in demand, such as accounting and law.

What are the three things in life you are most proud of?
Proud to be Omani. Proud of my family, who all supported me through my difficult times and my husband, who supports me always with his positive thoughts. Proud of being the only C level woman in Omantel.

Who would you identify as your role model? Whom do you look up to and why?
My previous bosses in Omantel were great mentors and motivated me to excel. Apart,

Chief Audit Executive / Omantel

I attended one of the leadership simulations by Dr Michael Khouly, in which he spoke about setting up a purpose and looking towards it as you progress. His books also inspired me subsequently.

If you had extra time of four hours a day, what would you do during that time?
I would spend more time with my family, and I would participate in charitable organisations and sports.

How would you describe yourself in three words? Do you live with a daily routine, and what is your secret to success?
Honest, self-motivated, love to see others happy. I work with honesty and openness. I have also worked on turning negative situations into positive ones - at the personal level and at work. Positive thoughts bring positive energy.

Did the Omani culture you grew up in have an impact on your career path?
Yes. The culture I grew up in has positively impacted my career as I grew up independent and given decision-making space. But I am also a firm believer that respecting society, culture, and tradition are very important for women's success. Omani culture supports women's education and career growth.

What is your favourite place in Oman, that you like to visit in order to relax and recharge your batteries?
The beach - looking at the sea and the horizon, having a walk or just coffee in front of the beach energises me. Jabal Akhdar, see the beautiful nature and cold weather.

Umaima Al Mahdhori

What was the best piece of advice that you were given regarding your career and that you will never forget?
My father's advice has two aspects: "Appreciate your work and take your work goals as seriously and equally as your personal goals. Think about this as a representation of who you are".

What has shaped you the most in your life? Is there any specific situation?
Wrong choices and decisions helped me a lot to develop. I always believed that only intelligent people could learn from their mistakes, turn them into opportunities for positive change, and adopt healthy habits, relations, better goals, attitudes, and mature life perspectives.

On the path to where you are now, what was the most determining step?
Deciding to utilise the maximum of the capacity of my brain and skills was very triggering for me, never to stop looking for opportunities.

What do you respect most in other successful women?
I always admire successful women who got to where they are from scratch and overcame many challenges and complicated circumstances. However, I noticed that most of the successful women did not get to where they are unless they realised and declared the challenges openly first, and then explored the way out of this by assertiveness and focus. I always admire women seeking more success and pursuing positive change for themselves, their families, society, and their country.

What would you recommend to a student just starting and dreaming of a successful career?
I always tell students and job seekers I meet as part of start-ups consulting and training to find their passion and keep learning. These two aspects are ultimately linked; when you keep learning about everything in life, you will find your passion and where you want to go in life and your career.

What essential qualifications do you think will be needed ten years from now?
It might not be an academic or a professional certificate. It might become a trait that you were born with or a skill you can develop by learning and practising over the year. I always considered analytical thinking and reasoning as two top timeless skills. However, suppose a person wants to take it to a leadership level.

In that case, they might think that developing an additional unique set of attributes and skills like linking with influential people, emotional and social intelligence and a good level of cognitive abilities would be a perfect blend for leaders' success.

Founder / The Planners Projects

How would you describe your leadership style? What is your leadership motivation?
My leadership style is based on the "growing together as a team" philosophy. I believe in the power of team support and how it helps every team member achieve, grow and feel satisfied.

Which topics should humanity focus more on in the future?
Smart urbanisation, advanced education accessible by all, sustainable natural resources, entrepreneurial and innovative teaching, more localised research and development (R & R & R&D), open economic and supportive business ecosystem, attracting external investment.

What does it take to be a successful woman these days? What are the three top things successful business people should personalise?
Patience, persistence, and commitment are the right blend for every successful professional, woman or man. However, they all should consider that getting committed to any successful business or career, achieving success in it would have a set of sacrifices called "Opportunity Cost" such as; time, money, relations or even the night sleep sometimes.

Did the Omani culture you grew up in have an impact on your career path?
I grew up in a family that appreciates education and believes in the importance of continuous learning and taking development opportunities. Moreover, we have in Oman the right environment, good social acceptance, and proper supportive regulations for Omani women to contribute to building this country and upcoming generations, which is a true motivation for every Omani lady to take the opportunity to achieve her ambitions.

(Dr.) Yasmin Al Bulushi

On the path to where you are now, what was the most determining step?
Taking risks, though I try to take calculated risks!

Who would you identify as your role model? Whom do you look up to and why?
My mother - positive, patient, resilient and confident. She has always infused the love of learning and excelling in any dimension of life. Moreover, she always showed respect and welcomed others' views, emphasising the importance of treating people how we want them to treat us. This was reflected later in my leadership style.

What would you recommend to a student just starting and dreaming of a successful career?
Enjoying the process (the journey, not only the destination). Making mistakes is part of the learning process. Be curious; try to learn from every opportunity. Connect to your community and network (students, support centres, teachers, sport mates, etc.).

If the entire world listened to you for five minutes, what would you say or what would you want to talk about?
I believe that we are all leaders as we lead our lives. Leadership is about decision making, what, how, and more importantly, the "why". If we look closely behind our choices, we find that they depend on our emotions. We can all perform better if we pay attention to our feelings, reactions, understanding others' feelings around us, and being cautious of our vision and goal.

What essential qualifications do you think will be needed ten years from now?
Leading with Emotional Intelligence in the Artificial intelligence era!

How would you describe your leadership style? What is your leadership motivation?
I don't think I have one leadership style that I stick to. If I need to motivate my team and help them to improve, I tend to use coaching.

Project Manager / Eitmad (National Leadership Project)

At times, the transformational leadership style is necessary to focus on strategic vision & drive performance/progress. Sometimes, before taking a significant decision, I use the democratic or participative style, where I value the views of all team members.

What are the three things in life you are most proud of?
I am proud of bringing positive change in many people's lives, starting with my family, community, or professional life. I am proud of the trust, being known and respected for the work and contributions I make and proud of what I achieved based on hard work and dedication. I am pleased overall to be recognised by others, looking at every opportunity in life as a learning and growing option.

Which topics should humanity focus more on in the future?
As basic as they sound: leadership, communication, empathy, optimism, and connection are more complicated as we move digital.

What does it take to be a successful woman these days? What are the three top things successful business people should personalise?
Patience, resilience, being empathetic, networking (connections) and being willing to take risks yet staying humble.

Is there a quote you favour that suits you? Or an important book you read that influenced you?
"Leadership is about making others better as a result of your presence and making sure that impact lasts in your absence", by Sheryl Sanberg, COO of Facebook.

How would you describe yourself in three words? Do you live with a daily routine, and what is your secret to success?
I live my life off-balance on purpose. My daily routine is not very systematic, and it greatly depends on "priorities". In the middle of all the hectic work, I do not forget to take time for myself and my family.

Did the Omani culture you grew up in have an impact on your career path?
Yes, the Omani culture emphasises "acceptance and diversity". I worked with people coming from diverse backgrounds, ethnic groups, locations and religions. It helped me accept the difference and connect with various communities around us, exchanging their thoughts, ideas, culture, and experience. We also have the "shura", consulting others who are experienced, getting different perspectives and feedback before making significant decisions. The Omani culture is also focused on "respect", so primarily we work with others on a high level of respect and appreciation.

What is your favourite place in Oman, that you like to visit in order to relax and recharge your batteries?
I love the long shores of the Sultanate. The great landscape that Oman is gifted with is the breathtaking scenery of mountains in Jabal Al Akhdar, the desert in Wahiba sands, and many beaches.

Zahra Al Harmali

What was the best piece of advice that you were given regarding your career and that you will never forget?
"If your skin is soft, go home!"

What has shaped you the most in your life? Is there any specific situation?
My charity work and involving myself with people who are struggling mentally and physically.

On the path to where you are now, what was the most determining step?
Establishing the first private, non-profitable organisation in Oman, as it is a struggle to keep it afloat.

Who would you identify as your role model? Whom do you look up to and why?
Prophet Mohammed (PBUH), my parents, Nelson Mandela and Gandhi, because they deeply cared for others.

What do you respect most in other successful women?
Their hard work.

What would you recommend to a student just starting and dreaming of a successful career?
Take as much advice as you can, and don't be scared to make mistakes, as it helps shape you into a successful person!

If the entire world listened to you for five minutes, what would you say or what would you want to talk about?
Love and respect are the keys to peace!

What essential qualifications do you think will be needed ten years from now?
Raise awareness on drug addiction among our community, analysing a drug addict to provide better treatment and encourage family support.

How would you describe your leadership style? What is your leadership motivation?
Coach leadership style, that we achieve better results when we come together.

If there is a lot of work and you are under stress, how do you compensate?
Family time!

What are the three things in life you are most proud of?
My family, my success and my religion.

Do you do anything to keep you fit physically or mentally, and how often?
Yes, walking and meditation, and I do it every day!

CEO / Shuroq Al Amal Al Alamia

Which topics should humanity focus more on in the future?
Drug addiction and its struggles.

What does it take to be a successful woman these days? What are the three top things successful
business people should personalise?
Courage, knowledge and respect.

What would you devote your time and energy to if you were to invest now, in your future
best self?
In self-development, to be able to assist my patients better.

Is there a quote you favour that suits
 you? Or an important book you read that influenced you?
"I can't, but we can."

If you had extra time of four hours a day, what would you do during that time?
I'd spend more family time.

What are your most important goals?
Is there is a difference for you between life
goals and career goals?
There is a difference between the two; my
career goals are to serve both genders in my
community. As for my life goal, I wish to
further my education on my specialisation.

How would you describe yourself in three
words? Do you live with a daily routine?
I do not live within a routine. I am proactive,
sufficient and eager.

Did the Omani culture you grew up in have
an impact on your career path?
Yes, it has shaped my career in a sense, as
this issue is considered taboo in our culture.

What is your favourite place in Oman,
that you like to visit in order to relax and
recharge your batteries?
Staying in hotels and resorts, strolling in
Mutrah and my mother's place.

Zainab Al Harrasi

What has shaped you the most in your life? Is there any specific situation?
My disability is what shaped me. Since I was six years old, I have been physically handicapped; I lost the ability to walk and move my body. Then, when I was 22 years old, I got an infection in my lungs, which led to the need to use a ventilator through the tracheostomy. Since that time, I have realized that I am different and distinct from my peers. I don't have the luxury of being an ordinary person if I want to have a great life.

Therefore, I have to work hard to achieve my dreams and struggle at every stage of my life. Whenever I suffer a health crisis and my physical strength declines due to deteriorating health conditions and staying in the hospital for a long time, I come out with a more vital spirit and high energy to strive and not give in to any obstacle facing me. So I keep moving forward to become what I want.

On the path to where you are now, what was the most determining step?
I have two decisive steps in my life, and I am proud that I made the right decisions. Firstly, when I joined Sultan Qaboos University to study for a bachelor's degree, my first desire was to study in the College of Science. Still, the university refused at first on the pretext that the College of Science does not accept students with disabilities and that I must register in another college. However, I was confident that I could study scientific disciplines, even if I had a severe disability.

I could write by holding the pen in my mouth, and I knew that I could adapt to the nature of the study. So I refused to study in another college and insisted on my position. Then the university agreed to give me this opportunity, and after that, the College of Science started accepting students with disabilities.

Master Student / Podcast Initiator

Secondly, after four years and three months of using a ventilator, I travelled to Germany hoping to breathe without the ventilator and close the tracheostomy. The doctors told me that my lungs couldn't breathe without a ventilator, and I needed it for my whole life. I felt that I could breathe normally without needing a machine, so I asked the doctors to give me a chance to gradually breathe independently of the device.

They agreed to let me try, although they were not convinced. After a month, I was able to dispense the ventilator completely, and after two days of writing these words, the tracheotomy will be closed, and I will return to Oman without machines. I think, If I gave up at that moment, I might have lived my whole life breathing through a ventilator and facing all the challenges that come with it.

What do you respect most in other successful women?
A woman's strength, ambition, constant quest to achieve her goals, sacrifice to achieve her dreams, serving her country, community participation, and sharing her experience with young people to inspire them is what I respect and appreciate in women.

If the entire world listened to you for five minutes, what would you say or what would you want to talk about?
If I have 5 minutes to talk to the world, I would like to tell people to hold on to their dreams even if it seems impossible and there are many struggles. They have to believe in themselves, and they can do their best to achieve their ambitions and not give up if someone tries to discourage them. Moreover, they must enjoy life so they can continue to strive.

Furthermore, I will talk about people with disabilities, their rights and the importance of empowering them in societies. People with disabilities can participate in various fields if they are provided with inclusive and equal opportunities.

What are the three things in life you are most proud of?
First, I am very proud and lucky to have a loving, caring and supportive family at every moment of my life. Secondly, I had the support of my Omani community as I was honoured by the venerable lady on Omani Women's Day 2020 among 50 persevering women. Third, I continue to work hard and persevere to this day despite all the challenges I have faced in my life.

Is there a quote you favour that suits you? Or an important book you read that influenced you?
I read the book "The Taste of Patience" by the Omani writer Mohammed Al-Oraimi, who talks about his experience with disability. It greatly influenced my life as I read it in a difficult time when I was desperate, and it helped me regain my energy and inspired me to find the "ellaws3ha" team. We created inspiration content on YouTube, where I shared my story and a podcast to share inspiring stories about the successful Omani youth.

Zakiya Talib Al Amri

What was the best piece of advice that you were given regarding your career and that you will never forget?
Never skip an opportunity to get experience and learn about other people's work in your organization. Instead, get familiar with doing as many tasks as possible to gain the knowledge and hold more responsibilities.

What has shaped you the most in your life? Is there any specific situation?
Going outside my comfort zone and seeking challenges without fear of failure. I seek different experiences either through the different organizations and sectors I've worked in and through the life challenges that were outside my comfort zone. It's enriching as I learn a lot about myself, capabilities, leadership styles, organizational cultures, and being agile, adept with changes, and considering adding value.

Fear of failure can be a significant obstacle to enrich the person's experience. However, failure is an outstanding teacher in life where we become less arrogant and more appreciative of our efforts in our journey to success.

Who would you identify as your role model? Whom do you look up to and why?
Admiring a person as a role model is basically admiring the values they embraced in the world. We seek to have/embrace different values as much as admire various role models. My mother is my 1st role model. She embraced the values of love to Oman, love to family, being strong during hardships and never stopping seeking knowledge.

What do you respect most in other successful women?
I do respect successful women who support and inspire others to be successful. The strength of any society starts with the women who inspire, support and uplift their own spirits and their surroundings.

What would you recommend to a student just starting and dreaming of a successful career?
Have a clear path to where you want to achieve and when you want to achieve it. Do not feel superior to do any work and get as much experience as you can. You will eventually learn. Seek mentorship from the beginning of your career, and don't be afraid of asking questions and seeking support from others, especially those who reach the same goal you want to achieve.

Do you do anything to keep you fit physically or mentally, and how often?
Physically, I exercise 1-2 hours at least four times a week, and I go for a 30 minutes evening walk in nature at least 3 times a week. I also make sure to follow a nourishing and mind-friendly diet with proper and quality sleep. Mentally, I keep myself fit through my meditation (control my mind and manifest my future), my reading (to widen my thoughts, ideas and

knowledge) and journaling rituals (to understand my thoughts, feelings and to realign my compass to focus on my current aims).

Which topics should humanity focus more on in the future?
Learning How to Learn; to keep yourself sharp in any area you seek to have more knowledge and depth in. Learning How to Write; to have the ability to reflect your thoughts and ideas and share knowledge with your community interested in the same.
Learning How to Meditate and Manifest; strengthening your mind, re-centre and ground yourself, and imagining your future. This tool will give you the power to recharge, sustain and have agility through your journey, regardless of hardships.

What does it take to be a successful woman these days? What are the three top things successful business people should personalise?
To live and embrace: maintaining focus, paying consistent efforts and sustaining change.

What would you devote your time and energy to if you were to invest now, in your future best self?
Investing in learning how to manage your energy is the base to keep yourself sustainable and able to absorb the knowledge you acquire in the various fields, including the ones related to your profession, new technological trends, etc. I believe that understanding how energy works within you will help you strive for more knowledge and will let you add more value to society.

Is there a quote you favour that suits you? Or an important book you read that influenced you?
"Your remedy is within you, but you do not sense it. Your sickness is from you, but you do not perceive it. You presume you are a small entity, but within you is enfolded the entire universe. You are indeed the Evident Book, by whose alphabet the Hidden becomes Manifest. Therefore, you have no need to look beyond yourself. What you seek is within you, if only you reflect." (By Imam Ali Bin Abi Talib)

What is your favourite place in Oman, that you like to visit in order to relax and recharge your batteries?
I find peace in mountains and nature. Mountains always inspire me with their wisdom, strength, profound silence, and truth.

Zuwaina Al Rashdi

What was the best piece of advice that you were given regarding your career and that you will never forget?
To always keep going and follow my passion.

What has shaped you the most in your life? Is there any specific situation?
When I decided to start my own business, be free from my corporate job, leave the corporate world, and become my own boss, this took so much courage and was an important decision I took in my life, which now is what I love to do.

On the path to where you are now, what was the most determining step?
Leaving my high standard corporate job and focusing on my business. This is by far the most challenging decision that I took. It was much work where I grew, and I am genuinely grateful that I did.

Who would you identify as your role model? Whom do you look up to and why?
His Majesty Sultan Qaboos Bin Said. I look up to him because he provided us with the opportunities and built the base foundation for us to grow and flourish - for the whole Sultanate of Oman and the women in particular.

What do you respect most in other successful women?
Their commitment to strive towards success and the way they support each other in their fields.

What would you recommend to a student just starting and dreaming of a successful career?
To follow their passion! That is what will pay off in the future.
If there is a lot of work and you are under stress, how do you compensate?
Being with my family and surrounding myself with loved ones.

CEO / World of Handicrafts

What are the three things in life you are most proud of?
- My Family.
- My Career Path (My Corporate Achievements).
- My Company and Organization.

Do you do anything to keep you fit physically or mentally, and how often?
Unfortunately, no, I don't do anything regularly. However, I do like to go for a walk now and then with my kids.

Which topics should humanity focus more on in the future?
I am convinced that the digital world is evolving now and will grow in the future even further on digital marketing and online ads. In my opinion, that is very important.

If you had extra time of four hours a day, what would you do during that time?
I want to exercise and take care of my physical and mental health.

What are your most important goals? Is there a difference for you between life goals and career goals?
My life goals and careers are considered united. My main goal is to reach the international market. I want to ensure that the Omani Handicrafts products are represented globally and will be known for their beauty and heritage.

How would you describe yourself in three words? Do you live with a daily routine, and what is your secret to success?
Yes, I have a daily routine that I go by. I would describe myself as patient, creative, ambitious. What makes me successful is that I go after what I want and learn from my mistakes.

Did the Omani culture you grew up in have an impact on your career path?
Yes, The Omani culture impacted my career path. It is what shaped me and made me reach this far. The products I take care of, Omani Handicrafts, show my deep respect and love for the country.

What is your favourite place in Oman, that you like to visit in order to relax and recharge your batteries?
Jabal Al-Akher, it's such a beautiful place, and I located one of my shops in the Al-Anantara Hotel.

Thank you!

This book has taken me on a fantastic journey over the past year, and there is a whole team of people to whom I am eternally grateful, not only for their support but also for their continuous hard work behind the scenes.

Firstly, I would like to thank my family, who truly supported me by allowing me to work all hours of the day and night and for their understanding and respect for this book project. It is such a good feeling to have loved ones by your side that you can rely on, trust, and allow yourself to be yourself.

I have great respect for and truly appreciate all of the women who participated in this book, and I am very grateful for their trust and honesty in answering the questions. This support especially humbles me as I could not travel to Oman and meet these amazing women personally. I sincerely enjoyed all of our communication, be it on the phone, video call, WhatsApp, email or anything else. I look forward to seeing our paths crossing again in the future.

My special thanks go to Ms Malak Al Shaibani, Dr Lamya Adnan Al Haj, as well as Ms Shatha Maskiry for their tremendous support from the beginning. Thanks to Ms Sumaiya Al Wahaibi for inviting me as a speaker. Let us continue to EMPOWER!

My graphic designer, Julia Bitschi has stayed the course with me during the whole process, no matter how many changes came in again and again and again – thank you also for implementing all of my ideas exactly as I wanted them from the beginning and for always being friendly, appreciative and in a good mood!

My editor Fiona Simpson-Stöber, thanks for your insights and also for all of your editing and calming me down when it became hectic in the end. I truly appreciate you being the only actual native speaker within this project and supporting it as you did.

Mazoon Printing, Oman, I would like to thank you for all of your time and your fast and reliable responses and for releasing this project with incredible speed and professionalism.

Photograph of Oman

Firstly, I would like to express my gratitude to the Ministry of Heritage and Tourism in Oman for providing such amazing pictures of Oman. The copyright and sole ownership of all pictures of Oman in this book remain by the Ministry of Heritage and Tourism in Oman.

Cover photo

Katrin Zeidler Photography, Ueberlingen, Germany

Photography credits portraits of successful women

Sincere thanks to all participating successful Omani women for providing and allowing me to use their photographs.

Credits in alphabetical order:

Afan Al Harassi	Mohammed Al Harthy
Ahmed Abdullah AL Ruwashdi	Nawaf Al Busaidi
Brandin Company	Pascal Mannaerts
Eymard Estanislao	Reality CG
Firas Abduwani	round.om
giuliafrigieri.com	Sara Al Alawi
Hilal Al-Badi	Saghroon
Hilal Art	Sarah Hale from Booma
Imad Hasan Photography	Talal Al Hasani
layal photography	Yiming Weng
Khalid Al Busaidi	Yuliya Photography
Maha al Zaabi	Zahran Al Abdulsalam

Lightning Source UK Ltd.
"on Keynes UK
√010832251121
ɔ85UK00011B/583